FREDERICK LEE BRIDELL

(1830-63)

C. AITCHISON HULL

Matador
9 De Montfort Mews
Leicester LE1 7FW, UK
Tel: (+44) 116 255 9311 / 9312
Email: books@troubador.co.uk
Web: www.troubador.co.uk/matador

ISBN 978-1906221-096

Front cover: *The Coliseum at Rome by Moonlight* (courtesy of Bridgeman Art Library)
Henry Rose (1925-1905), William Havell (1782-1857);
Elizabeth Barrett Browning (1806-61); James Duffield Harding (1797-1863)

Frontispiece. Portrait of the artist (courtesy of Southampton Arts & Heritage Service)

Typeset in 12pt Bembo by Troubador Publishing Ltd, Leicester, UK
Printed in the UK by The Cromwell Press Ltd, Trowbridge, Wilts, UK

Matador is an imprint of Troubador Publishing Ltd

To Dr. J. Sweetman. PhD.FRSA.
ex Fine Art Department,
Southampton University.

~ CONTENTS ~

~ ACKNOWLEDGEMENTS ~

Southampton Arts and Heritage Services, for the reproduction of the Bridell photograph (frontispiece). Albert Cooper for supply of later photograph of Bridell.

Mr David Cousins for his generous reproductions of the above photograph.

Margaret Christian, and library members of Christies's for help in the early days of my research. The staff at West Yorkshire Archives in Leeds.

Dr. J.A.V. Chapple for permission to reproduce from Letters from Mrs.Gaskell.

Reading Art Gallery for the help with information on William Havell and the supply of images. The Fine Art Society, London. The Berg Collection in the New York Public Library for permission to reproduce a letter of Elizabeth Barrett-Browning. Dr Philip Kelley, Wedgestone Press, Waco. Texas, for additional information. My grateful thanks also to a private collector for the provision of images and permission to reproduce them.

Finally, I would like to record my gratitude to Dr. John Sweetman, now retired, of Southampton University Fine Arts Department for his interest and support. His original article in *Apollo* added impetus to this endeavour, and his subsequent suggestions added insight and clarity to the narrative.

~ FOREWORD ~

In 1970, Southampton Art Gallery, had in its regular exhibition a large canvas entitled *The Coliseum at Rome, by Moonlight*. The work is impressive in its depiction of the ancient ruin dramatically outlined against a moonlit sky. The artist had chosen a particularly bold rendering of the subject which highlights the triumph and decay of a once powerful empire. It is a grand concept on a grand scale. As we look more closely at the work in order to make out the shapes and figures moving through the murky shadows, we become aware that the artist had an immensity of vision which stands starkly in contrast with that of many of his contemporaries.

The label at the base of the painting provides a little further information: 'Frederick Lee Bridell. 1830-1863'. Southampton Art Gallery has numerous other items, in the collection by the artist, but none as impressive as *The Coliseum*. These are woodland and lake scenes, and are evidence of the painter's visit to the continent. There are also some small portraits in oils and pencil sketches. These depicted working people, boats and artefacts such as a traveller would note when pausing for a while on a journey. We can glean from the reference books, additional information on the artist and the nature of his work. *The Dictionary of Victorian Painters* by Christopher Wood (1975) describes Bridell as:

> 'Landscape painter. Apprenticed to an art dealer he travelled round Europe painting copies for him. After visiting Italy returned to England and settled at Maidenhead. Exhibited at the RA 1851 and 1862 also at the British Institution and Suffolk Street. Subjects are all continental views especially Italy. Returning to Rome, he married E Fox who exhibited at the Royal Academy in 1859-1871. Had Bridell lived longer he might have become a considerable artist but his output was too small for him ever to achieve lasting fame.'

In August 1974, an article appeared in *Apollo* by Dr. John Sweetman, of the Fine Art Department of Southampton University, entitled 'F L Bridell and Romantic Landscape'. Dr. Sweetman pinpoints the heroic quality of Bridell's Romanticism and places him in the aftermath of Rosa, Byron and Goethe. In addition, the artist is also looking forward with the vision of Turner beside him. The artist, placed at this juncture was greatly influenced by the Classical past and the Dutch school of landscape painting. 'In the scope of his vision, and the atmospheric movement depicted in The Coliseum, he follows in the footsteps of Turner. His serious painting shows him to have been an artist of talent and potential'. In reviewing the scope and density of Bridell's achievement, Dr. Sweetman calls for a re-evaluation of Bridell's work. He states that a one-man show for this artist is overdue.

In 1975, Southampton Art Gallery assembled an exhibition entitled 'Frederick Lee Bridell'[1] which displayed items of the artist's portfolio that were in the Art Gallery's collection. A later exhibition in 1968, entitled 'Viewpoints'[2] by The Fine Art Society in London included in their exhibition of landscapes, four works by Bridell.

A letter to The Southampton Times appearing on the 14th Jan. 1888, from the printer and engraver Henry Rose, provides us with valuable insight into Bridell's life. Without doubt, Rose believed his friend to be a genius, from the days when he first began to sketch as a boy. Writing some twenty-five years after Bridell's death, his remembrance of certain facts was apt to be slightly erroneous but nevertheless the letters, a second one printed the following week, give interesting details of Bridell's early life. Those who had known him and wrote of him following his death accorded greatness to him for which he justly deserved recognition. Sir Theodore Martin wrote of him as a man who would have been one of England's greatest artists had he lived longer.[3] And Graham Reynolds in Victorian Painting records 'his early death seems to have robbed mid-nineteenth century English landscape of an individual note.'[4]

In marshalling the facts regarding this artist and his work, there are a considerable number of intriguing questions which have arisen. Primarily, difficulties surround the number of works that were produced with the same title and/or very similar subject matter. Bridell often completed two or more studies for larger works which, in themselves, were completed pictures. Those depicting Lake Como are a particular instance of this problem. In addition, not all of his works were signed by him and it may be the case that signatures were added later, by another hand. Queries have also arisen over authenticity. It is a consideration, that works initiated by Bridell could have been completed by another hand, and these do not stand up to close scrutiny. One or two works also bear erroneous dates or dubious signatures. Hence the catalogue of completed works is, by its nature, a flexible tool and not a definitive listing. The main area of enquiry however concerns the present location some of his major works.

There has been no trace of diaries, from Bridell or his wife. Richard Garnett records that Bridell kept notebooks of his travels and these 'testified he was completely absorbed by his art of poetic landscape.'[5] It also appears that there are no known images of Bridell's wife, which is surprising, given that she was a portrait artist and had artist friends. The only likeness surviving her death was a miniature portrait of herself (and her second husband) bequeathed to Beatrice Smallfield, a painter and daughter of a Royal Academician. There appears to be very little surviving evidence of Eliza Bridell-Fox's long painting career, apart from the portrait of her father, William Johnson Fox in the National Portrait Gallery collection. With regard to Bridell's apprenticeship and employment, it is possible that Edwin Holder may have retained documents and letters which were passed to the Holder family by his daughter. It would be of significant interest if any of these or related items were now brought to light, to add to our knowledge of this hitherto forgotten artist.

The recent growth in information technology is providing opportunity for the discovery of further additions to the catalogue of the artist's work. It is interesting to note that the recent acquisition by Southampton Museums of *Landscape around Southampton* 1855 was returned from Australia. In Milan in 2005, Sothebys[6] sold an item entitled *Twilight at Abbadia Lariana* which has not been seen publicly and was very likely to have been sold directly by the artist to a buyer in Italy. The catalogue of works compiled at the end of this book is largely based on sale records. There are, quite clearly, far more works by Bridell than realised by the writers of reference articles on the artist. Additionally, many of the works that were produced from sketches in Bavaria have never been to auction. It is to be hoped that the discovery of further pictures will add impetus to the rediscovery of the genius of Bridell. One might hope for the opportunity for the public to see his range of output, especially examples of his major later works, as a fitting tribute to the artist.

The main aim of this biography is to awaken an interest in the work of this artist and accord recognition for the achievement of his short life. From humble origins he dedicated himself to art and produced works of great sensitivity and power. Arising from my personal interest in the artist, this booklet reflects an interest in the social changes which occurred in the Victorian period and an appreciation of the movements within the wider world of art. In recording what is known of Bridell's life, I have endeavoured to set it in the context of the times.

Lee Bridell was baptised William Frederick Bridle in Southampton in
December, 1830. His father, John Bridle, was a carpenter from Gillingham in Dorset, who was
born in 1799. John Bridle's mother, Bridell's grandmother, Jane Lee, died a few weeks after
her son's birth, and was buried at Bere Regis in Dorset. The name Bridle is found frequently
in records of the early nineteenth century in the Dorset area, predominantly in Weymouth,
Dorchester, and Poole. In 1841 there were two families of this name in the St Mary's Ward of
Southampton who had migrated to the expanding town from the rural countryside. John
Bridle's second marriage (following the death of his first wife) took place in Millbrook in 1824.
His second wife was born Amelia Brown in 1795 in Christchurch, Hampshire and is referred
to on the record of their marriage as Amelia Brown Bartlett.

In his letter to the *Southampton Times* of 14th Jan.1888, Henry Rose provides an interesting
sketch of Bridell's father:

> 'His father was a carpenter, and one who thought that whatever a man was he
> should be thorough and do his work in the best possible manner. The father was
> for a great number of years a valued foreman to Mr.T.C.Elliott, of Northam; he
> still lives close by, and is eighty-eight years of age. I called on him on Sunday last,
> and found him reading, without spectacles, a well-thumbed small Bible, and, to
> use his own words, he was quite ready for the call to "the eternal home." In
> conversation his old vigour and enthusiasm again showed itself, and no one who
> could have heard him would have felt any surprise that he was the father of a great
> genius.'

The admiration that Rose had for both Bridell and his father is evident. It further provides us
with an inkling of the influence that he would have had on his son. If there was some
inherited factor in Bridell's artistic capability, it would seem that Rose was not aware of it.

John and Amelia's first daughter Jane was born in 1825. The second daughter Mary Ann was
born in 1828. William Frederick, their last child, was born 7th November 1830, and baptised

at St Mary's Church on 5th December of that year. *The Southern Evening Echo* of September 10th 1983 published a photograph of a house in Houndwell, describing it as the house where he was born. His baptismal certificate states his place of residence as Houndwell. Further notes in the newspaper article identify the location as the 'next house but one south of Chapel Street', and Henry Rose confirms this as adjoining the Park[7]. Accommodation in this period was rarely taken on a long-term basis, and very often the deciding factor was proximity to the wage earner's location of work. Two years after the birth of William, Jane died aged seven years and the death was recorded in Craven Street. In 1841, mother, father and the two children were residing in Pope's Buildings, which were tenement blocks on St. Mary's Road. The early years for Bridell were dominated by privation in what was then a very crowded and unhealthy area of Southampton.

During this period, large-scale changes in social conditions were precipitated by the development of the port of Southampton and the consequent increase in population residing in the town. Despite the recent expansion of housing in the St Mary's area, between the old town and the River Itchen, there was intense overcrowding within the older parts of the town. By 1851 the population was just over 34,000 and approximately 23,000 of these were living within St Mary's Ward. By 1861 this figure was 27,500. As with other large towns, the wake of the rapid expansion was followed by problems of public health. These problems, though often in the process of being addressed by the public bodies, were more forcibly addressed in the wake of epidemics, particularly those of cholera. This was an 'imported' disease, and ports in particular were the areas most seriously affected.

Three major epidemics occurred, the first in 1848, then 1853 and finally in 1866. Following the epidemic of 1848, a committee was formed to identify the problem areas of Southampton. In Houndwell, the Royal Hotel waste was not draining away. By 1849 the inspector for the Public Board of Health in Southampton, a William Ranger, started an investigation. His report listed overflowing middens, privies that had not been emptied for fifteen years and common lodging houses where ventilation was provided by the removal of a brick from the wall. There was the continuing nuisance of the old canal at Houndwell, which had not been filled in. This ambitious proposal for a canal had been made at the end of the 18th century with the aim of linking Northam Quay and the Town Quay with Salisbury and ultimately London. It had become however, a stagnant ditch owing to lack of use. In 1841 an old woman fell into the canal and drowned and it was proposed then that it should be filled in. Work commenced in 1846 with the spoil from the excavation for the railway tunnel. Problems continued to plague this project as part of the railway tunnel collapsed into the original canal, which at one point passed underneath it.

The railway had a major impact on the prosperity of the town. In June of 1839 the final link between Southampton and Basingstoke was opened, and journeys to the terminus at Nine

Chapel Street

Elms in London were available. The first class trains could complete the journey in three hours. The single first class fare was 20/- per passenger and 13/- for servants, who were to be in livery in order to discourage fraud. Thus the wealthy were able to afford the benefits of the steam train. For the less wealthy, there were two goods trucks a day. These were open trucks, the fare was 7/- and the journey took six hours.

By 1841 the only coach company running a daily service to London was the Red Rover. The coach service had, in 1838, thirteen coaches per day each way to London.

The coaching business was in decline and coach building, which had been the town's main industry for two generations, was redundant. It was the docks which benefited directly from the railway, and the work on the building of the docks began in August 1839. There was some anxiety at first that the presence of the navvies, about 1000 in 1841 and then 1600 before the dock was finished, might lead to an increase in crime and violence: but these fears proved groundless. By 1842 a large tidal dock had been completed which contained 18 feet of water at the lowest tide. It was accessible to steamers of 2,000 tons and at high water to almost any vessel. Southampton's future fortune as a major port for goods and passengers was sealed. In 1840 the first National School for St Mary's parish was built in Grove Street and Fred Bridle, as he was then known, received basic schooling during these years.

During this early period, Bridell made the acquaintance of Henry Rose. Rose was older by six years and also took an interest in art. Later he was to become a printer and engraver, remaining in business in Southampton until the early 1900's. Rose, later, in what can be described as a twist of fate, was to have a decisive influence on Bridell's career.

> 'When Bridell was eight or nine years of age a picture of a ship he had drawn attracted my notice, and I said "Fred, I did not know you practised drawing." He replied. "I have never done any before; this is my first attempt."[7] I encouraged him to do more, and lent him copies; and he soon gave his whole soul to the work and improved rapidly.' Bridell left school at about the age of eleven or twelve years and commenced work in the town. Henry Rose's letter provides further details regarding these early formative years[8].

> 'I think he must have left school at a very early age, and commenced 'doing' to earn a livelihood. He had one voyage in a coasting vessel, which satisfied any desire he had for a sea life. He was then page boy to Messrs Corfe and Sampson, surgeons; afterwards working for at least three house painters in the town. At fourteen he could grain and marble as well as many.'

This letter also provides us with insight into the development of Bridell the artist.

> 'He was always studying nature with open eyes to pictorial effect, every cloud or tree or rippling wave leaving its impress on his marvellous memory. At this time of his life he used for a change to write poetry, tales, &c., coloured by the same vivid imagination which afterwards made poems of his pictures'

The 'marvellous memory', commented on by Rose, was to be one of his greatest assets as a painter. Additionally, we are told of Bridell's natural leaning towards poetry. In this he frequently added some of his own description to a picture, which suggests that for him poetry and painting went hand in hand as complementary aspects, in the description of nature.

> 'When he was about fifteen I tried to get him included in a mutual drawing class in which two young professional artists – Mr. William Baron and Mr. William Burgess – myself, and three or four enthusiastic amateurs used to meet twice a

week to practice drawing for personal and mutual improvement; but I was for some time unsuccessful, as they said "we do not meet to teach boys, but to help each other." After some time, however, they gave in; young Bridell formed one of our little coterie, and soon showed that he could do more than his share for the general help'.

Subsequently, the following week, Henry Rose furnishes further detail regarding a drawing class which Bridell was 'allowed' to join. This interesting letter provides some colourful background to the social situation of these times.

21/01/1888
'In my letter last week upon Mr. Bridell, I spoke of a mutual drawing class composed of about half a dozen of us. Permit me to add a few lines and say that we used to meet at the house and by the earnest request of Mr. Philip Carter, mattress maker No.2&3 The Strand.

Mr. Carter was known to the public as an ardent Chartist who harangued large assemblies in the Park from the elevation afforded by a chair, generally getting very excited himself and impressing his hearers with the same feelings. His vehemence often got him into scrapes and once before the magistrates. He was a tall man, of great energy and generally walked as though he had conscientious reasons for doing four to five miles an hour. He had no school education; in his early life he was engaged in tending sheep on Salisbury Plain, driving the plough &c. He used to tell thrilling stories of privations and hardships he had gone through, but he had educated himself and his mind was well stored with general knowledge. Our experience of him was that he was a gentleman of fine feeling, tender susceptibilities, generous impulses, keen appreciation of the beautiful and true, and possessing a passionate love for the fine arts, especially drawing and painting, in which he showed great ability, his pictures testifying that he was a real artist. He was an enthusiast, and did much to inspire us in the sentiment and practice of art. He agitated for the establishment here of a Government School of Art, which doubtless had its influence in the fulfilment of his desires.

Of those of us who met at his house, only Mr. William Burgess of Manitoba (a letter from whom to me appeared in the Independent of the 4th inst) and myself remain. We hold an ever grateful and abiding sense of the help and inspiration we received from Philip Carter, the eccentric mattress maker of the Strand.'

The Chartist movement in Southampton was part of the wave of working class discontent, which centred on the larger industrial towns of the north and Wales. Beginning in the late

1830's the main aim of the movement was to gain acceptance of The Charter by Parliament. In essence, this was to obtain a vote for every man and allow industrial action through trade unionism. Southampton did not have the same degree of industrialisation as some of the larger towns of the north, where the craftsmen, the new poor, were being replaced by power driven machinery. Consequently, although there were public meetings, which gave rise to disorder, the movement was not able to enlist the support of adequate numbers to lend much impact to the movement in the South. Writers who addressed their concern over these social and political questions were numerous. Charles Dickens and Mrs. Gaskell were amongst those whose writings were effective in highlighting the plight of the disaffected poor.

As a house painter, Bridell, according to the nature of the work, would have had to mix his own paint from raw materials. This experience was invaluable to him in his acquisition of technique. He would have developed an understanding of the qualities of the pigments, their permanence, stability, and how they reacted and flowed with the addition of a medium. As Rose records in his second letter, 'He studied the nature of various pigments and mediums in reference to their abiding qualities, the effect of which even in his early paintings renders them as fresh today almost as the day they were painted.' He was also a competent watercolourist, and life was becoming easier, for the watercolour painter. Easily transportable metal tubes containing paint were introduced by Winsor and Newton in 1852. Bridell was also rapidly gaining in technical competence, as testified to by Rose. We are told that he was extraordinarily talented. A talent which was inherent and not an acquired skill.

> 'Bridell worked for house painters, among whom were Mr.Martin, who lived in a cottage where Misselbrook's grocer's shop now is in East-street; Mr. Greenwood, French-street; and, lastly, Mr.Davis at Northam, the closing scene of which was this; – Bridell had prepared a room for graining, when Mr.Davis told him he could grain the window and skirting, but he would do the doors. Bridell said he should do all or none; he did not mind preparing for his own graining, but would not for others. The upshot of which was that his house painting had reached its finale, and he commenced portrait painting, one of his first being a small portrait of myself.' [9]

Thus Bridell was precipitated, with minimal tutoring, into his future career, initially, as a portrait painter. His own conviction of his talent and future destiny and also an awakening maturity instigated this change of affairs. The small portrait referred to by Rose, now in Southampton Art Gallery, was completed in November 1848. On the reverse it is inscribed 'Portrait of Henry Rose/painted by his friend/Frederick Lee Bridell/November/1848'. William Frederick had become Frederick Lee. The 'Lee' adopted from his grandmother's maiden name.[10]

★ ★ ★

Another one of these early portraits in oils, that of Mrs Gilfroy, an unknown sitter, is in the domain of Southampton Art Gallery. Mrs Gilfroy was the wife of a shoemaker who resided in Northam Street, a neighbour of his father's employer. Henry Rose, by this time an engraver and printer, had set up a small business at Above Bar, Southampton. He recalls[11] that one day, an artist called Mr Holder came in to order some cards to advertise his rates for portrait painting – with rates running up to 180 guineas. Henry Rose, impressed with these sums and assuming the gentleman to be a consummate artist, in conversation, told him of his friend who had begun portrait painting. He fetched the nearly finished portrait of himself as he wished to have Holder's opinion and in his own words 'he anticipated a grand future for my friend'. Holder was immediately impressed, the more so when he learned that the artist was entirely self-taught. He declared that he could not paint so well adding 'there is genius of the highest order' and requested an introduction to the artist. Consequently, an appointment was arranged. The outcome was indeed fortunate, at least at this early stage of his career, for Bridell. Initially, for three years, Mr. Holder was to pay all of the artist's expenses, in return for all of his pictures and then a further percentage was to be paid to the artist upon the sale of his work. The arrangement was promising. It offered the opportunity for study and travel, and a guarantee against adverse circumstances. Though initially advantageous to Bridell, the artist could not foresee the restrictions that would evolve from the arrangement. It was necessary, at the inception of an apprenticeship, for a premium to be paid on behalf of the apprentice. How much this was at this time is difficult to assess, but from information passed on by Mr Holder it would seem it was paid by his father.

Of the earliest commissions of his apprenticeship, a pair of portraits of Mr and Mrs Day have been recently acquired by the Maritime Museum, Southampton. Completed in 1850, they depict two members of a prominent family. Mr W. Summers, owner of the Millbrook Foundry had acquired partners in 1834, a Mr John Groves, and Charles Arthur Day. The names of Summers and Day remained connected to the Northam shipyard until its closure in 1929. The two portraits, painted for the sum of £2.16s each, however, reflect an important change in the patronage of art in the Victorian era. The artist was no longer dependent upon the landed gentry for commissions to depict their families or residences. It was now the newly wealthy, the merchants and the factory owners, from whom the artist sought patronage.

Freed from the necessity of portrait painting, the artist turned his attention to his overriding passion, as we learn from Henry Rose, that of landscape. He had completed, in 1849 a *View of Southampton* in oils, which is now in Southampton Art Gallery. This picture reveals the competence of Bridell, at the age of 18. The sky shows the developing raincloud, over the harbour at Southampton. The cloud heightens the last of the sun spreading across the harbour. In the foreground the figures of fishermen, grouped with a small dog, indicate the artist's attention to detail, even in his earliest work. The motif of a group accompanied by an animal or animals, is found throughout his later work. It is in the overall composition, however, that we discover the balance and harmony that is the keynote of this artist.

Portrait of Henry Rose
Courtesy of Southampton Art Gallery

By 1851 the income of Bridell's family was such that they were at this time tenants of a newly built house at 17 Millbank, as recorded in the census of that year. Several years later, in 1855, Mary Ann Bridle married a widower and removed to East Street. She gave birth to three daughters: Lydia (1854), Lizzie (1856) and Elsie (1858). We can reasonably assume that Bridell was in contact with his sister and her children, certainly the older ones, and may have made some contribution to the rise in the family's fortunes. His parents continued to reside in this area, and moved, at a later date to 2 Millbank. Here Bridell's mother died in 1879 and his father in 1892 at the age of 91.

Bridell's new employer, Edwin Holder, was the son of a Yorkshire artist Edward Holder (1783-1865). Edward had been born in Burlington in Yorkshire in 1783 and spent his life in the Yorkshire area. His son was an aspiring artist, but did not possess the talent to follow in his father's footsteps. He painted small tableau de genre works, still lifes and farmyard scenes, which he exhibited at Suffolk Street between 1856 and 1864 and later at the Liverpool Academy and British Institution between 1859 and 1862.

His occupation was as a picture restorer. In this capacity he travelled the country and worked for notable gentlemen in Lincolnshire, Chichester, and London. For a period during the early 1840's he restored paintings for Sir Charles Winn of Nostell Priory in Yorkshire. Letters from Holder to Sir Charles, in the Leeds Archives, provide details of the paintings he was working on at various times during a ten year period – a Claude, 4 works by Salvator Rosa, 3 by Richard Wilson, 4 by Van de Velde and a portrait by Sir Peter Lely. He also advised on the acquisition and sale of pictures, suggesting sums which may be realised at auction.

Another, more successful Yorkshire artist, Edward H. Holder, was his cousin. He chiefly painted landscape subjects, in various locations in England. His son, of the same name, born in 1848, followed in his father's footsteps. As the son became more prosperous, he took up residence in Reigate, with his wife and ten children in 1891.

A year after the beginning of his apprenticeship, Bridell was residing near Maidenhead, Berkshire, at a cottage in Holyport. Living with Holder, his wife and daughter Charlotte, this was for Bridell undoubtedly an improvement in living conditions and environment. The picturesque village housed a few cottages, and was accessible to Reading and the River Thames. Surrounded by fields and forests there was little comparison to the crowded and unhealthy conditions he had experienced in Southampton. Charlotte, the same age as Bridell, submitted four of her pictures to various exhibitions and followed the life of a painter. At thirty years of age she was residing with her parents in Yorkshire and described herself as a 'student in painting'. She was studying then at the York School of Art, and in the Annual Exhibition of 1864, she is highly commended. Did Edwin Holder cherish the hope of such a talented youth becoming his son-in-law? He probably did. At all events, she never married but continued at her father's business for all of her working life.

Bridell is recorded on the census of 1851 as Frederick Bridell and described under occupation, as 'apprentice to artist in oil painting'. The details record that he has defective hearing, possibly due to a childhood illness. Rose provides a little further information with respect to his physical characteristics. He was 'rather above middle height, of slight build, of a warm, enthusiastic temperament, and massive brain. No hatter could furnish him with a hat except by having it specially made.'

Working in the vicinity of Maidenhead, the young artist is painting and drawing river scenes, and exhibits his first major work *A Bit in Berkshire* in 1851 at the Royal Academy. Henry Rose also records a smaller work, *Entrance to the port of Havre* being exhibited in Suffolk Street at the Society of British Artists, and selling on the first day for 12 guineas.

He was developing his sketching technique and laying the groundwork for his preferred method of working. It seems that, after selecting his subject, he sketched in pencil and added watercolour. He did work on occasions with pen and ink and at times gouache, but these were not his usual methods of 'taking notes' for his studies. He could complete several sketches in a day and would work on them later. From these sketches, he often completed a study in oils. From this study, at some time – it may have been several years later– the larger and final work

9

was completed in oils. At a later date, he may have returned to these studies, which he retained, in order to complete a commission.

During this time in Berkshire, Bridell became acquainted with a family of artists and engravers resident in Reading named Havell. Members of this family also lived close by to Holyport, in Bray. William Havell (1782-1857) had been a founder member of the Old Water Colour Society. As a young man, he had established himself as a most impressive painter of watercolour landscapes. Indeed he was a strongly independent individual with definite and lofty aims, as he stated:

> 'My first desire as an English Landscape Painter, is to represent my own beautiful country without referring to other painters, ancient or modern; my next, is to paint the splendour of daylight and sun-shine, the glory of Art and Nature.'[12]

He was considered by some however as an abrasive and arrogant character. In 1808 he suffered criticism from a foremost patron of the times, Sir George Beaumont, who had written to Wordsworth as follows:

> 'I think the drawing you mentioned to me of Havell's one of the best there – he has however lost his breadth and upon the whole been retrograde.'[13]

Sales of his work following the criticism began to decrease. However the end to the wars with Napoleon in 1815 had brought economic and social problems in its wake. Returning soldiers caused a rapid rise in unemployment. There was a downturn in the markets generally which had an unavoidable impact on the art market. Havell sought means to make a viable living.

He departed for China as official artist to Lord Amherst's embassy in 1816. The embassy's mission was to promote British mercantile interests, but it was unsuccessful, and Havell spent eight years from 1819 in India. Returning to England, where little had improved in the interim, he struggled to make a living and decided to venture to Rome. He returned to England in 1830, after staying for a period with Thomas Uwins, a fellow member of the Old Water Colour Society, near Naples. However, he was not a healthy man, surviving fever and cholera during his years in India. He was an artist who painted in both watercolour and oil, but remained throughout his life a member of the Watercolour Society, exhibiting there from 1825 until 1856, sending one of his final works, *The Waterfall* to the Royal Academy in 1856.

Of William's brothers, George, Edmund and Frederick achieved notable recognition as artists or engravers. William's brother, Edmund, a painter, was drawing master at Reading School. His son, Edmund Havell Jnr. (1819-1894) was also a painter in portraiture and sporting scenes. A competent artist, he may have provided Bridell with instruction and accompanied him on

William Havell
Courtesy of Reading Art Gallery

joint sketching expeditions. He had completed a portrait of Elizabeth Barrett Browning in 1847 and thereafter became fairly prosperous. Taking a house in London, in later years, he also became the official portrait artist for Queen Victoria.

In certain motifs in Bridell's work we can see links with the work of William Havell. A wide vista receding to distant hills typifies many of Havell's compositions. Havell's overriding conviction in his work was that the great aim in landscape art was to enable the spectator to see into space and that this could only be done by a perfect knowledge of light. *A View near Rome* by Havell of 1828 contains elements which are characteristic of a Bridell landscape. The goatherder, in the foreground, pipes to his flock. This was a theme Bridell adopted for *In the Campagna* and *Fiume Latte, Lake Lecco*. There is a vast spaciousness of view in Havell's compositions which frequently contain references to antiquity, very often in the foreground there are remains of ruins. In the far distance the receding hills overlook the Campagna. From Havell's *Plains of Sorrento* which was engraved by his brother, we can immediately identify the adoption of plant motif and harvesting tools which Bridell displays in *A Neapolitan Landscape*. The work was in fact, attributed initially to Havell, until the signature was clearly identified.

Temple of Vesta

Havell had also illustrated a subject from the poem by Spenser, *The Faerie Queene*, depicting a setting entitled *Una and the Lion*. Bridell was also very much inspired by this particular poem and the settings that its imaginative descriptions gave rise to. In 1850, Bridell completed an imaginative work *The Temple of Vesta*. This may have been inspired by William Havell's painting of *The Temple of the Tiburtine Sibyl*, which had been engraved by his youngest brother F. J. Havell. (F. J. Havell had died in 1840, at a relatively young age, after a complete mental breakdown.) The engraving was executed soon after William had returned from his 1829 visit to Italy.

Bridell's viewpoint, taken from a lower level than that employed by Havell, has echoes of the same scene by Abraham Louis Ducros. (J.M.W. Turner had the privilege of access, and was undoubtedly influenced by these large watercolours at Stourhead). Havell presents the lush scenery in which the Temple rests dramatically on its high point, overlooking the place where the Sibyl is bathing. It was an area which was very popular with artists working around Rome, and is described by the Reverend Headley in his *Letters from Italy* 1845.

'The chief waterfall of the Arno is full in view, a little to the left on the other side of the gulf. Right out from the green hills it leaps 100ft into the mass of verdure below. It is a spot of singular wildness and beauty. At length we reach the Grotto of Neptune, a black cavern into which the cataract formerly emptied itself from the high wall of rock above it. From this deep gulf the view of the Sibylline Temple standing in its beautiful proportion high above, the massive rocks around, the singing of the waterfall in our ears – combined to render if for the moment a scene of enchantment.'

The young artist based his imaginative interpretation on the engraving, but was equally inspired by Spenser's description. Already, in this vast detailed composition we see evidence of Bridell's natural competence in the depiction of vast areas of mountainous landscape. The movement of the light through the work takes us into the scene. We are glimpsing the idyllic pastimes of the nymphs, in a timeless setting. A distant plume of smoke signifies life on the hillside. This was a favourite motif of the artist and frequently employed in his later scenes from the Bavarian Highlands. The work (49x34ins) presents a consummate marriage of mythology, reference to the Classical past in the Temple on the hilltop, and the landscape. The landscape, not here presented as backdrop for the characters, has its own identifiable forms which convey a sense of realism to the work. Bridell has also, in this work, tackled the naked human form with a natural competence. The figures, seemingly belong to the landscape are not overstated or merely there for decorative effect. The grouping of figures, and animals, in all his works is a subject for close attention. His unfailing sense of pictorial effect comes to the fore, and a pervading sense of completeness arises from his choice of pose and size of the group. The studies for this work were to be the subject for a later, grander, painting. It was to be ten years later that he was to visit Tivoli and complete a work, *The Grotto of Neptune* from the actual setting.

Bridell continued to copy from subjects, probably suggested by Holder, both paintings and engravings. Readily available also was the *Liber Studiorum* by Turner, a collection of engravings of different branches of landscape art. It is likely that the artist visited the galleries of London, and also copied works in private collections. Sir Theodore Martin is remembered for his contribution to literature as a translator. In later years he became a personal friend of Queen Victoria, staying at Osborne House with his wife on many occasions. He allowed Bridell to copy in his private collection, and the introduction may have been through Bridell's connection with Edmund Havell Jnr.

In the National Gallery were works by Claude and other great landscape artists, and these were regularly augmented by the acquisition of works of the Old Masters from Italy.It was not until 1853 that he was able to see Turner's paintings *Dido building Carthage* and *Sun rising through Vapour*. Turner had specified in his will that these were to be hung alongside the works of Claude in the National Gallery and the request had been approved by December 1852.

Engravings were also available to the landscape artist. These were produced to meet the rapidly growing interest in travel. In effect these were the travel brochures of the day, and part of Turner's purpose in travelling to the Continent was to acquire sketches and subjects for engraving. David Roberts, an Academician since 1841, was one of the foremost topographical painters of the time. His albums of lithographs of the Holy Land and Egypt published between 1842 and 1849 made his fortune. Many landscape artists had their roots in this very lucrative area of mass-produced images. Bridell had a rich market on which to draw inspiration. *The Tourist in Italy* had been produced in 1832, and comprised engravings of drawings by the artist James Duffield Harding (1797-1863),who was an important influence on Bridell.

Harding, the son of a painter, was born in Deptford. It was intended that he follow a career in law, but his talent came to the fore at the age of 13 when he exhibited at the Royal Academy. He became a student there for a short period and took drawing lessons from Samuel Prout. He was then apprenticed to the engraver John Pye, who was on friendly terms with Havell for most of his life. However, Harding could not settle to the work and deciding on a career as an artist, he went to Antwerp. For two years he was a student in a school run by the Belgian artist, Baron Wappers, thereafter returning initially to Hastings. During the following years he made several trips to Italy and toured throughout the Continent, making pictures for engraving, and specialising in what can be described as the 'continental picturesque'. By this time he had become one of foremost drawing masters of the time and Ruskin was one of his pupils, from 1841.

Ruskin in *The Lamp of Beauty* thus describes his tutor:

> J. D. Harding, brilliant and vigorous, and clear in light as nature's own sunshine – deep in knowledge, exquisite in feeling of every form that nature falls into –[14]

Harding's far reaching influence, particularly in his teaching of art and its principles is now lost in obscurity. After his death he was remembered for his development of the lithotint, which allowed for the gradation of tones and brushwork to be successfully reproduced. Two articles in the Art Journal provide us with evidence of his dedication to the teaching of art and his struggle to achieve recognition. Fortunately, his books remain as documentation to the clarity of his thought. He was an artist who believed in the direct observation of nature and also that artists should be capable of capturing the atmosphere of a scene through careful study.

James Duffield Harding

In common with other watercolourists, he produced drawing manuals as an additional source of income. David Cox, as early as 1811, had produced *A Series of Progressive Lessons* for the watercolourist, that were extremely popular. Roscoe's *The Landscape Annuals* (1830-9) were followed by Harding's *Elementary Art* (1834) and *Lessons on Trees* (1852). His most comprehensive manual appeared in 1845, entitled *The Principles and Practice of Art* in which he set down his beliefs that 'Art has not and cannot have any other basis than Nature.' It is pertinent to recall that at the heart of the teaching at the Royal Academy was the study of the Old Masters. Intensive copying and analysis was its focus and Harding was forthright in his approach to this method of acquiring technique:

'In treating now of Imitation with respect to the employment of composition, light-and-shade and colour, I have offered nothing which depends for its authority on myself, or on the practice of any school at any period. My object has been to explain truths which are ever-existent in Nature, to derive from them the principles of art and to show how those principles are to be carried into practice.' He adopted the same stance as Ruskin ; and later, with reference to the treatment of Nature: 'I urged on the student the importance and superiority of

15

that kind of imitation which is mental rather than mechanical – which endeavours to express what the artist feels when viewing his subject as a whole, rather than minutely copy that which he can only see when intently looking at a single part.'[15]

Uppermost in Harding's artistic expression was his attention to the important aspect of composition, termed the 'picturesque.' Originally, as Gilpin had noted in 1792 in *Three Essays*, this idea was applied to the forms of nature, and denoted an object or view as worthy of being included in a picture.

'But among the objects of art the picturesque eye is perhaps most inquisitive after the elegant relics of ancient architecture; the ruined tower, the Gothic arch, the remains of castles and abbeys. These are the richest legacies of art. They are consecrated by time; and almost deserve the veneration we pay to the works of nature itself.' Harding accentuates the importance of the picturesque and in his critical view, some of the Old Masters are deficient in this aspect of composition.

In style entirely distinct from Turner, Harding, in his more ambitious works, focused on the rendering of space and aerial perspective. His studied compositions incorporated an expanded sphere of vision and reflected nature in all her varied moods. This was executed in drawing by any means at hand, or painting, such was his versatility in any medium. His works combined a delicate balance of sensivity and and boldness of interpretation. It is very likely that Bridell adopted Harding's opinions regarding the 'picturesque', having the same spaciousness and depth in composition, but retaining close attention to detail. The comments in The Art Journal regarding Harding's talent for figurework can equally be accorded to Bridell.

> 'There is another feature that distinguishes his works above those of most landscape painters, and that is, the introduction of his figures; they are always, whether of the human or the brute creation, most cleverly drawn, easy picturesque, natural, and ever in their right places; even his solitary places are rarely deserted."[16]

We read the comments regarding the review of Harding's work in the 1851 Exhibition (illus):

> 'From point to point the eye ranges resting here and there upon considerable objects rendered minute by distance, the whole enclosed by the everlasting Alps. Definitions of distance are rendered by the utmost delicacy. This work is a production of rare excellence.'[17]

In the early 1840's, Harding adopted painting in oils and endeavoured to become a member of the Royal Academy. He was unsuccessful in his attempt and in 1856, returned to the Society of Painters in Watercolour. Harding, like other artists, struggled in his endeavour to enter the hallowed circles of the Royal Academy. But it was necessary firstly to be elected to the position of an Associate member of the Royal Academy. The number of these members was limited to twenty. The number of full members of the Royal Academy was limited to forty. When one of these died, resigned or retired, his successor was elected from the ranks of the Associates. John Linnell, whom it was agreed by the President, Eastlake, had demonstrated his ability as an artist, submitted his name but was passed over at least twenty times. Finally, he withdrew his application but it was not a reflection on the artist. The 'cloak and dagger' methods of the Academicians increasingly came under scrutiny. The Committee and its practices inevitably came up against stern criticism in the media. A pamphlet of 1860, describes the Academy in the following manner (sic):

> 'The association in Trafalgar-square is a close body in every sense of the term. Its deliberations and acts are shrouded in the strictest secrecy; and if perchance, in spite of the jealous gard that is maintained, any information thereon oozes out, the Royal Academicians are considerably disconfited, as in the recent publication of the list of candidates for the Associateship. In the competitions for its honours, the non-exhibition of the candidates' specimens, the witholding of information from the press, and the general secrecy that is observed, create dissatisfaction and distrust.'[18]

Notwithstanding, the failure to achieve the security and status of a Royal Academician, Harding did have the trappings of a well-to-do Victorian gentleman. He owned a house in the fashionable area of St.John's Wood, and his own carriage and horses. Following his death in 1864, the Art Journal editor recorded his indignation in Harding's obituary of March 1865:

> 'How it was that the talents and labours of Mr.Harding were never recognised by the Royal Academy is one of those strange facts the mysteries of which it is impossible for one outside of the building, to penetrate.'

The writer amplifies the achievement of Harding:

> 'An artist with a world-wide reputation, earned in a field where energy and perseverance were allied with genius, a man of action, possessing large sympathies with Art and artists, with a mind full also, of varied information, a gentleman in every sense of the word– such a man would have reflected lustre on the Academy as great, if not greater, that the Academy could confer on him.'

As one of his pupils noted, he was 'on one hand greatly admired and on the other, as much misunderstood and unappreciated.'[19] (see appendix).

Harding became a full member of the Society of Painters in Water Colour in 1821, exhibiting there regularly until 1846. During the period of the 1830s, he would have known and had contact with William Havell, but this connection may have been from an earlier date. William Havell, during the summer of 1812 had stayed with his sister in Hastings. Coincidentally, Harding sent a *View of an old house Hastings* to the Royal Academy in 1813. There may have been a link between the two artists, dating back to these early days.

Havell was also a great friend of John Pye, the engraver, to whom Harding had been apprenticed for a short period. There is additional evidence of a connection from Harding's work entitled *Hurdwar – The Gate of Vishnoo*, a scene in India, it was engraved by F. J. Havell in 1837. Additionally, the sale from Harding's studio after his death included a work by Havell, entitled *An English River Scene*, and it is possible that it had been given to him by the artist.

Bridell owned and read Ruskin's *Modern Painters*, volume 1 of which had been published in 1843. This treatise was part of a monumental work which Ruskin worked on over a period of seventeen years. He addressed very thoroughly the manner and purpose of art and related his thoughts to the past and present expression by major artists. He makes sporadic references to Harding in this work, and refers to Harding's 'most fearless, firm and unerring drawing.' One of Harding's pupils, Walker, had also absorbed his lessons. When the first volume of Ruskin's work appeared he did not hesitate to state that 'old pupils recognise in an amplified and elaborated form, some of his lessons.'[20] Since Ruskin would have been influenced by Harding from his contact with him and vice versa, interesting comparisons and considerations of influence arise.[21]

Harding provided practical instruction, backed by clear and simple theory. The principles are evident in Bridell's work and suggest very close links with his thought. It is speculation that Bridell was fortunate at some time of having lessons from Harding. Harding did give drawing lessons, but these were in the main, to ladies of the gentry. And we know that Harding sketched in the vicinity of the Thames, submitting a work entitled *View on the banks of the Thames at Maidenhead* to the Royal Academy in 1856. The overriding influence of Harding is nevertheless evident in the motifs in Bridell's work which indicate his close study of Harding's manuals.

★ ★ ★

In December of 1851 Turner died. The will was not settled until 1856 owing to confusion between which works qualified as sketches and which as finished work. A legal case ensued in order to settle the matter. Lady Eastlake declared it to be 'a very stupid will – that of a man who lived out of the world of sense and public opinion.' She found it incomprehensible that he should 'leave his own daughter not a penny, but his housekeeper gets 150*l*. a year.'[22] John Ruskin, a great supporter of Turner, following this settlement, proposed to undertake the cataloguing of his drawings, a task which was to take him two years. Turner's bequest was finally completed in 1857, his paintings then becoming housed in the recently opened Malborough House. Ruskin, in his self appointed role of critic and connoisseur, followed his *Modern Painters* of 1843 with his *Academy Notes 1855 to 1859*. As the interpreter of contemporary art his opinions were a dominant influence, greatly contributing to the fortunes of Turner and the Pre-Raphaelites by his support of them.

At the time of Turner's death, Charles Eastlake (1793-1865) had been president of the Royal Academy for the previous season and remained so until his death in 1865. He agreed to Ruskin's offer via an intermediary as the two men 'did not see eye to eye'. Jeremy Maas describes Eastlake as ' a kindly and scholarly if somewhat retiring figure who wielded power by virtue of his high office; it was no easy matter for an artist to make his way in the world without taking into consideration how he stood in relation to the Royal Academy and its deeply entrenched attitudes'.[23] In due course, Eastlake was also appointed Director of the National Gallery and the demands of the two positions left him little time for painting. He continued however, to regularly visit the Continent in order to acquire works for the National Gallery.

Turner, not without his critics, was generally acknowledged to be the greatest English artist of the period, but it was the Pre-Raphaelite Brotherhood, formed in 1848, who were attracting attention. William Rossetti gave this account of them:

> 'They entertained a hearty contempt for much of the art-flimsy, frivolous, and conventional – which they saw in practice around them; and wanted to show forth what was in them in the way of solid and fresh thought or invention, personal observation, and the intimate study of and strict adherence to Nature'.[24]

In their the united hope to regenerate art, they looked back to the purity and truth in the manner of painting of artists before Raphael. William Bell Scott described the movement:

> 'Like many ardent movements initiated by young men, it was all rather muddled, but no less vigorous for that'.[25]

The Brotherhood comprised Millais, Holman-Hunt, Dante Gabriel Rossetti, Woolner (a sculptor), James Collinson and Rossetti's brother, William who became secretary to the group. Also a member was Frederic George Stephens, a painter who took up writing on art and became the editor of *The Athenaeum*. Although the original members of the Brotherhood tended to follow separate paths a few years later, the impetus and influence of the movement permeated art for several decades. In keeping with new movements in art, they attracted much derision and press reviews which were particularly vitriolic. *The Times* recorded this opinion of the Pre-Raphaelites on May 3rd 1851:

'Their faith seems to consist in an absolute contempt for perspective and the known laws of light and shade, an aversion to beauty in every shape, and a singular devotion to the minute accidents of their subjects, including or rather seeking out every excess of sharpness and deformity. Mr Millais, Mr Hunt, Mr Collins and in some degree Mr Brown, the author of a huge picture of Chaucer, have undertaken to reform the arts on these principles. The Council of the Academy, acting in a spirit of toleration and indulgence to young artists have now allowed these extravagances to disgrace their walls for the past three years; ....though we cannot prevent men who are capable of better things from wasting their talents on uglieness and conceit.....'

Millais, who was born in Southampton in 1829, exhibited three paintings in the R.A. in 1850. One of these *Christ in the House of His Parents* did not receive the same acclaim from the critics as that accorded to it by William Rossetti, and much public debate followed. In August of that year, Ruskin came to their defence in his pamphlet entitled *Pre-Raphaelitism*. Ruskin was to come to their defence again in 1857, when a dispute arose at the Liverpool Academy. This concerned an award of £50 which was given annually to the best picture of the annual exhibition, as judged by the members. In this case it was Millais' *The Blind Girl*. *The Spectator* of January 1858 records as follows:

The Liverpool press, and a large section, at any rate, of the Liverpool public, dislike Pre-Raphaelitism, and the Academy is severely taken to task for its selection.'

In response to the opposition to the Academy's decision, which was threatening its future, Ruskin wrote to *The Times*. 15/1/1858.

'Let the Academy be broken up on the quarrel; let the Liverpool people buy whatever rubbish they have a mind to; and when they see, which in time they will, that it is rubbish, and find, as they will, every Pre-Raphaelite picture gradually advance in influence and in value, you will be acknowledged to have borne witness all the more noble and useful, because it seemed to end in discomfiture; though it will not end in discomfiture...Since Turner's death, I consider that any average work from the hand of any of the four leaders of Pre-Raphaelitism, Rossetti, Millais, Hunt, John Lewis, is singly worth at least three of any other pictures whatever by living painters.'

In due course, a small group broke away to form the Liverpool Society of Fine Art and Bridell was to exhibit here in 1861 and 1862.

★ ★ ★

Away from London and the continuing controversy over the PreRaphaelites, Bridell followed his own direction. He was not influenced by the current trends, resolutely keeping to the truths of his own perception of Nature. His early influences indicate that he looked in particular at paintings of the Dutch School. During the period 1850 to 1852, his output appears to be small and it is assumed that he was aiding his employer in restoration work. He may have continued with portraits, which was a reliably lucrative undertaking. But there is no evidence to confirm this view at the present time. Working in the region of the Thames, the artist's interest in river scenes was developing. The theme of water, in lakes and rivers was one that Bridell continued to explore throughout his work. He produced a few works in the vicinity of the Thames, for example *The Herons Home* and *English Landscape*. Although he did submit a work entitled *A Bit in Berkshire* to the Royal Academy in 1851, it appears that the work was overlooked by the reviewer for the *Art Journal*. He also completed a portrait of his employer, Edwin Holder (illus), which is now in a private collection.

Other works from this period are experimental in subject matter, and the majority of them are on a small scale. However he began to work in a larger format as evidenced from his painting *Autumn Evening*. The central main figure, on horseback, is suggestive of Cuyp and the foreground and vegetation has close resemblance to the work of David Cox. The man shown lying in the darkened foreground has been robbed and left by the wayside. It is a rare instance of a narrative subject by the artist, and seems to be largely an experimental work. Unusually, Bridell portrays the human figure in the prone position in the foreground (an idea he may have gleaned from Harding's Principles and Practice of Art). Essentially the picture comprises of an arrangement of separate successful parts into a contrived whole.

In 1853, his contract with Holder was renewed for seven years, on condition Bridell left England to study on the Continent. He visited the Louvre and during his short stay made copies of works by Titian and Dughet.[26] He travelled on to Munich, where drawing and life classes were freely available to art students. Bridell pursued his interest in landscape, extending his knowledge of the Flemish School. He was particularly interested in works by Cuyp, Jan Both and Berchem. Berchem, in particular, had painted and etched hundreds of idyllic landscapes in the German border country and also visited Italy. His motifs, a shepherd playing his flute, accompanied by his goats, and sometimes a dog, find strong echoes in the pastoral scenes of Bridell. We can glean the other influences and impressions that were of particular interest to Bridell by an examination of the works that were sold from his studio in February 1864: female peasants and cattle after a picture by Berchem in Munich; boats in a breeze after

Van de Velde; a peasant girl with sheep in a landscape after Gainsborough. The artist also copied at different times, the works of Wouvermans and Greuze, who was a figurative painter, and painters of the English school, Wilson, Pyne and Prout.

On the Continent, as in England, the Romantic movement represented a new perception of creative expression in response to new freedom. It had developed in France in opposition to the Neo-Classical approach with its association with the culture of antiquity and a depiction of outer perfection which stood as a metaphor for inner worth. The Romantics, in contrast, were open to the imperfect, uncontrolled aspects of nature. They were interested in the expression of emotion, not simply the expression of noble ideals. They were to use dramatic colour, freedom of gesture and emotive subjects. In effect they were breaking away from the restrictions of tradition. Firstly, from the stratification of subject matter, where previously history painting was deemed of the highest order and landscape the lowest. And secondly, landscape became important for its exploration of the personal response freed from the restrictions of the classical style. But this movement was not a sudden separation from tradition. The achievement of Claude was still in evidence, as Turner, the prime exponent, had shown at the beginning of the century, and continued to demonstrate in his efforts to depict British landscape subjects in Claudean mode.

In landscape painting at the beginning of the nineteenth century, two names stood out as the unquestioned masters, Gaspar Poussin, grand and majestic, and Claude Lorrain, who it was said 'had dipped his pencil in the golden hues of the sunshine'. Both had trodden the same path in search of the beautiful. As towering influences on landscape painters, Bridell was to take lessons from them in the scope and magnitude of his portrayals of nature but he was also to take account of Harding's view. Harding had stated that 'he was not one of those who believe the Old Masters, Dutch or Italian, are the exclusively excellent... In order to attain a high degree of excellence, something more than such a study is required. Nature puts in her claim to our attention. She is the great source of knowledge and feeling, and whoever neglects to seek inspiration at this source will never become a great artist.'[27]

It was Richard Wilson, the first British artist who was to look at nature afresh. In his sensitive treatment of the light, combining a truthfulness of colour he moved away from the ideal of classical construction. His fluent brush strokes captured the atmosphere and mood of the scene before him. Bridell followed in his footsteps. But what is evident also is the sheer breadth of Bridell's interest. He embraced the Classical past and the imagination and scope of Turner, but his response to Nature was not stylised or idealised. He competently tackled vast vistas but paid attention to the minutest of detail, without this attention impeding the over-riding sense of the whole. Reviewers of his work, when exhibited, described this quality as 'grandeur'. The compositional details form the parts of the ordered whole and result in a satisfying sense of completeness. But there is the unmistakable sense that the artist is seeking to capture not just

Morning Bavarian Highlands
Courtesy of Fine Art Society, London

the mood of nature, the scenery and its people, or his present experience; it is more than a faithful recording. He is engaged in a 'higher' scheme which echoes a timeless quality, a perception of the ideal within the commonplace and an expression of this quality where each aspect of life had an integral value set in the living environment of nature and time. Very often the ethos of the work's conception lay in poetic imagination. The observations were exact, but these given data are transformed by the imagination and the result is poetry, in its deepest sense. Turner's influence on Bridell is seen in the broad sweep. His compositions were bold, taking a close-up view or one which recorded a whole vista to the distant horizon. He aimed at conveying the feeling of a landscape, every picture inspired by a particular time of day which permeated the work through to the smallest detail. Sunrise, sunset, mist and moonlight provided the artist with the inspiration for the subjects in which he excelled.

As he travelled Bridell made small sketches of the working people he saw, the fishermen, the cattle herders, the shepherds, people gathering crops; the ordinary lives of the local people. Whilst journeying up the Rhine, as others who followed in Turner's footsteps had done, Bridell also spent some time completing drawings for later works. We know that he also visited Wallenstadt, St Goar, Heidelberg, Mayence, and worked on various sketches at the junction of the Moselle and the Rhine.

The artist was initially based in Munich. A small picture *Valley of the Inn Munich* indicates the simplicity in his subject matter and direct influence of the Dutch school. A peasant woman is washing clothing from a boat in the river. These smaller works were usually made in preparation for larger pictures. In this area near Munich it seems he completed several works with the title *Valley of the Inn*. The Inn is the river between Munich and Lake Chiemsee, which flows through Bavaria. This labelling gives rise to error as he did not always label pictures as such, but recorded them with a number on the reverse.(Some of these numbers were then removed on framing). All of the works during his apprenticeship were numbered and were probably used to list his output to Holder. We know that he also copied works in the Munich Gallery, in particular those of Berchem and Hackaert, and also exhibited at some stage in the city. He attracted a favourable comment in *The Munich Times*, which delighted him as he stated 'because firstly I am naturally proud of having won so favourable a remark from a foreign critic whom I didn't know.'[28] He became acquainted with the artists of the German school, Theodor von Piloty, Carl Rottmann and Schleich. Von Piloty followed in the tradition of history painting. In 1855, owing to his success with a work entitled *Seni by the Body of Wallenstein* he began to enjoy considerable recognition which allowed him to take a leading role in the art life of Munich. In 1856 he was appointed Professor of the Munich Academy and became an influential teacher.

Bridell was also developing an interest in wooded landscape subjects. Trees, solitary and in groups, often figured importantly in the composition, and, in some cases as the subject. They

FishermanHouse
Courtesy of Southampton Art Gallery

were identified by name and therefore became identifiable by the artist's study. He was particularly attracted to the beauty of certain trees. Neither did he set a scene with a backdrop, each part of the descriptive whole had its own identity. This accompanied a developing sensitivity to the effects of light. In *Munich* (23x19 ins) he depicts early sunlight casting its dramatic effect over the trees and rocks, casting into shadow a small foreground group of travellers. The passing travellers are not the central theme of the composition; nor are they incidental to it. The scene is topographically detailed and the figures, for this brief passage of time, part of the 'timeless ' grandeur of nature.

Another work, entitled *Morning Bavarian Highlands* (18x28ins. illus), similarly indicates a strong tonal range, and is convincing as a monochrome. The detail in the work has been very sensitively handled. The sweep of sunlight through the changing composition gives strength, depth and movement to the work. The dramatic theme of some of his work is lessened here, although there is a sense of attentiveness and impulsive movement in the group of foreground goats. One member of the group is perched on a high knoll as a lookout, anticipating possible danger. There is a very palpable sense of the animal straining for any unusual sound in the uninhabited valley.

These were the settings in which Bridell revelled. He was very likely not at home in town settings and made no works with towns as the subject. He probably left Munich for the country at every opportunity, seeking subjects that he found challenging, that of mountains and lakes illuminated by the changing effect of light.

Working from a village, Audorf, he produced sketches of the Wilde-Kaiser mountains. He then moved into the area of Lake Chiemsee, midway between Munich and Salzburg, completing landscapes near Altenmarkt and Brannenburg some 15 miles south west of Chiemsee, in 1854. In a letter he described the location for a subject of a large work (46x61 ins) entitled *Sunrise over Brannenburg* which was exhibited at the Liverpool Academy in 1856. He subsequently completed a copy as a commission and wrote a description, exactly as transcribed, of the area, to the then current owner of the painting in 1858.[29] The owner of this work, also had another painting by Bridell which shows a view of the same river (the river Inn) from another location. The letter reveals the artist's humour in his descriptions, particularly of the resident of the hermitage depicted in the painting. Rose has testified to Bridell's humour, describing him as being ' most genial, his ready wit and abounding humour and ever sparkling originality being an inspiration to any company.[30]

May 4 1858
Highfield Lodge
Southampton

This scene lies about two day's journey from Munich as such journeys are performed in diligence or Eil Waggon/haste waggon but which is nevertheless exceedingly slow. You ordinarily arrive there about evening and on the following morning (if a bright one) may witness such a scene as I have here portrayed. The little village upon the roofs of whose houses the rising sun directly scintilates, is the Brannenburg giving the name to the Picture.

Beyond it, rather to the right of it, and above it, is the mountain called the Matron a favourite resort of the deceived piety of the neighbourhood on account of a little chapel and Hermitage with a sanctimonious old vagabond residing in it, who cheats the simple peasants with assurances of his power to effectively intercede for all sorts of good and benefit to them, their corn and fruits and flocks, over which his Eiery(?) nest commands a view. Opposite the hermits home and to the right of the picture is the pointed mountain call the Herberg or Harvest Mountain. Though all the harvest I ever saw on it was few stunted patches of palid rye.

Between these two mountains that commence a glen here, and beyond them & immediately beneath the beams of the morning sun is the Wilde Kaiser or Wild Emperor Mountain celebrated (at least in this neighbourhood) as bearing in its peaks a resemblance to a colossal portrait of the Emperor Napoleon 1. This portrait however is not perceivable from our standing point and is indeed principally monopolised by the hermit and his visitors I never could see it myself at all–

The most distinctive and obvious character of the Forest growth all over the Bavarian mountains is such dense dark forests as that seen in the middle of this picture of a concave form beneath the sun and creeping up the sunny slopes of the mountain sides. The trees forming the forests are intermixed masses of the beautiful Fichte and Janne (both of the Fir tribe) it is a by no means desirable place to venture in unless on a decided road or pathway or accompanied by a mountain guide – I was once lost in such a forest though much farther from any habitation than this one, for nearly a whole day and only escaped by the strategy of following a goat track and faint and famished at such an escape from the dark and damp. (for it is always damp in these forests) a wandering was a great joy.the situation(?) is never to be forgotten, by myself or any other so situated.–

To tend the goats sheep and oxen on the lower Alp women are much more frequently employed in summertime in these Highlands than men are. And one of these is here seen in the foreground bringing fresh eggs and butter and a small flock of sheep down to the valley in which I forgot to mention before the water seen shining beneath the sun is the river Inn the same river as your first picture has in it. Though that view is some fifty miles further into the Highlands–

The low flat hut with stones on its rough wooden roof – on the little hill in the middle ground of the picture to the left where the smoke is seen emerging is very characteristic of the place. And nearer to you in front of the hut the trees under which the struggling sheep are clustering are young oaks whose foliage dies as September comes.'

This letter it seems, was written in some haste. The are some simple errors of spelling and very little in the way of clear formation of sentences. It does present an interesting picture of the artist being lost for nearly a whole day in the forest and without provisions, but it also indicates how Bridell took a keen interest in the flora and was attracted to its masses, referring to the trees as 'beautiful'.

Crossing the Alps via the Brenner Pass, he visited the area around Bolzano and Lake Constance. He also completed from these travels a work entitled *Vineyards in Meran*, now at Wolverhampton Art Gallery. All of the pictures the artist produced from this period went directly to Holder. Bridell returned to Southampton in 1855. Holder, it appears, was no longer residing near Reading and was engaged in setting up a printing business in Wakefield. In London there was much to excite public interest in art. Two names in particular were arousing wide public acclaim, William Powell Frith and Rosa Bonheur. (see Appendix).

It was during this year, that he was able to spend some time in his hometown and completed works from his German sketches. This was also the year of his sister's marriage and it may have been a family event that he returned for. It was also the year that Henry Rose's son was born. Bridell was continuing to receive commissions from patrons in Southampton and completed a pair of pictures *The Charcoal Burners* and *A Pine Forest on Fire for* the sum of fifty guineas each, from sketches he had made abroad. These subjects were popular and it seems he completed several similar versions on these themes. He was also a friend of Mr Wiseman, a frame-maker who custom-made frames according to the artist's specification. Mr Wiseman in due course also commissioned several pictures from the artist. Recently returned from Australia is the work entitled *View of Southampton* which had originally been in the ownership of the employer of Bridell's father. John Bridle was a foreman for T.C. Elliott, the owner of a large builder's merchants in Southampton in the nineteenth century. The work shows a view over the River Itchen and was completed during this year. It is a rare documentation of the changing face of Southampton due to industry and is at present located in the Maritime Museum. Other patrons for whom he completed works during this year were Mr Pearce of Highfield, Captain Strutt, Sir F.Perkins, Mr W.Brooks, Dr Clark and Mr R. Andrews (Mayor).[31]

★ ★ ★

Following completion of a pair of pictures for Mrs Wheeler, of Sussex-place (afterward Mrs Clark) – one *The Charcoal Burners* the other *A Pine Forest on Fire* – Rose, in his letter says 'I will mention a characteristic incident in this connection. On the completion of the first picture Mrs Wheeler sent Bridell a cheque for £50. This he brought to me for consultation on how to act. He said:

> "I engaged to paint the pictures for fifty guineas each – not commercial pounds and the loss of this 50/- would be off my commission."

He immediately wrote to Mrs Wheeler, reminding her of the artist guineas, and requesting the alteration the cheque, which received a prompt and favourable reply. These pictures were exhibited at the 1866 Exhibition at The Hartley Institute, and were then valued at £1,500.[32]

From this incident, it is clear that the artist was keenly aware of the percentage he received from the sale of his work. It is likely that he was considering freeing himself from the burden of an employer. In order to do this, he would have to buy himself out of the contract provided he was able to negotiate the settlement with a difficult employer.

In the summer of this year Bridell was sketching at Hythe in August, taking a trip to Windemere in the Lake District in mid-September and travelling back to Matlock in Derbyshire. Sketches from this visit were executed unusually, in pen and ink. Pictures from this trip include *Sunny Day, Derbyshire Hills, Matlock High Tor* and *Sunset on the Atlantic from Portland Bill*. There is also a major work *Grand Sunrise, Stonehenge* (50 x35ins) which later sold from the Bridell Gallery, and Bridell would have begun sketches for it at this time. It is another instance of one of the artist's paintings which has not been seen publicly. (It would be of interest to the author if this work is extant.) There is also evidence of Bridell touring parts of the country, as works completed include views of Portsmouth, Isle of Wight, Margate, and possibly Chester.

During 1856, Bridell relocated to London, where he had a studio at 17 Newman Street, London. This area was popular with artists since the turn of the century. 'Any painter, sculptor or architect who could afford a house – or a room – squeezed himself and his family into Newman Street or the network of streets around it'.[33] Ford Madox Brown had had a painting room in the same building from 1851 until 1854. It was probably the same room that Bridell took on. Brown provides us with graphic details of the events whilst he was working in his studio here. In 1851, he has Rosetti staying there with him on occasions:

> 'All this while Rossetti was staying at Newman Street with me – keeping me up till 4am – painting sometimes all night, making the whole place miserable and filthy, translating sonnets at breakfast working very hard & doing nothing'[34]

Here, he records in his diary for 1854, he began his work entitled *Christ Washing the feet of St Peter*. He also began a study from *Emma*, which he painted at night in Newman Street, but this work was not completed. There were artists and models at every turn in this small area of busy London. Edmund Havell also had a studio nearby in Berners Street from 1856-61. Bridell was possibly living and working in Newman Street, but visiting Holder, who was living in Isleworth with his family.

For artists, buyers and the viewing public, the centre for Art in England was the Royal Academy, and had been since its foundation in 1768. Most artists, as Harding had done, saw that full membership was the way to recognition and future security. It was the hope of every aspiring artist to exhibit at the yearly Exhibition, housed during these years in the building which is now the National Gallery. Another important centre was the British Institution, which had been founded in 1805, and was at the west end of Pall Mall. Lacking the prestige of the Royal Academy, it provided a much-needed addition to the facilities available to artists and buyers. Income came from the charging of an entrance fee and a five percent commission on sales. As Jeremy Maas describes, the 'mania for buying pictures by living artists, had taken hold by 1850…Clearly the old exhibiting institutions, the Royal Academy, The Society of British Artists, the British Institution and the two water-colour societies, although still generally respected, were not really adequate'. Moreover, 'they were hives of bumbledom with vested interests and totally proof against change'.[35] The situation gave rise to independent bodies with their own committees and they formulated their own rules. The first of these, the Free Exhibition was inaugurated in 1847 at the Egyptian Hall in Piccadilly.

Bridell had already exhibited at an earlier time at the Society of British Artists in Suffolk Street, which had been in existence since 1823. This society was popular with landscape artists. Here, as with the majority of exhibitions at the time, there was controversy over the way that pictures were hung. A cartoon in Punch of May 25th 1861 depicts a viewer standing on the shoulders of another viewer.

Strong feelings fuelled debate about the allocation of spaces for picture hanging. It was noted in the Art Journal in 1850 that one of Harding's best pictures was hung in the Architectural

Cartoon from 'Punch',
May 25th 1861

room at the Royal Academy exhibition.[36] By 1857 however, there were, according the editor of *The Athenaeum,* more that enough galleries and exhibitions. He loquaciously records the Society of British Artists exhibition of that year:

> 'This exhibition is scarcely needed. The Academy, the 2 Water Colours, the French, Flemish and German collections, the Portland Street and the British Institution are enough for all real men and all pretenders. All the plates of fish, sliced cucumbers, smiling dogs, portraits of gentlemen, simpering corpses, small – salad landscapes, smears and streakinesses, and spottinesses and daubs – may all be crowded into the other exhibitions.'[37]

Under Holder's direction Bridell prepared to exhibit, submitting the following year to the British Institute in February, the Royal Academy in May and the Liverpool Academy in September. There was of course, the increased interest in art from the new industrialists of the north. If we note the number of works exhibited in Liverpool by William Havell, it is clear that he believed more opportunities were to be had from the new industrialists, than in London. He exhibited there on average at least ten works each year between 1837 and 1857. He may have influenced Holder in this choice. Such displays promoted reviews and sometimes adverse criticism but were absolutely necessary for an artist to establish his reputation. He needed to make an impression if he wanted to command good prices for his work and establish himself as an artist.

At the British Institution he exhibited *Highland Loch Scene* and *Break of Day, Chiemsee, Bavaria.* He exhibited at the Royal Academy, *The Wilde-Kaiser Mountains* (location unknown) and *The Charcoal Burners*, the latter being loaned back to him by Mrs Wheeler. These pictures Henry Rose records were hung in very bad positions. At the Liverpool Academy he exhibited *Sunrise over Brannenburg* (location unknown) which was sold to a Mr Thomas Croft of Liverpool.

Once the summer exhibition of 1856 was finished, the picture *The Pine Forest on Fire* prompted Bridell to write to Mr. Mogford in order to locate and return the painting to its owner (sic):

> 17 Church Terrace
> Isleworth
>
> Nov 19 1856
>
> Sir,
> If you reflect you will credit me for sufficient patience. Having written about six weeks from this time of closing of the Summer Exhibition and have received as yet no notice of the how or where of obtaining my picture–

I learn with some concern that other artists have obtained their works from the Hanover Square rooms – I have sent several times there but cannot find anything of mine. The Picture is not my property but belongs to a Lady in Southampton who commissioned it and then kindly lent it to me (after paying for it) for Exhibition in your gallery.

This lady reading in the Papers that the Exhibition closed in October is becoming very solicitous for the repossession of her property. An I of course am unable to send her any satisfactory answer.

The Gentleman who kindly called for me at the Hanover Square rooms went afterward to the house of Mr Green but could not find any Picture among those in his charge – in this dilema which no fault of mine has created my only appeal is to yourself – to ensure as speedy an answer as possible I make a copy of this and send it to the Gallery.

The title of my Picture as I have before written "Charcoal burning at the foot of the Wilde Kaiser Mountain in the Bavarian Highlands".

Your prompt attention to this matter will greatly oblige
Sir!

Yours most obediently

F L Bridell

H Mogford Esq J.S.A.[38]

In due course, the work was returned to its owner.

The scope afforded by the landscape of Bavaria and northern Italy, was to inspire the artist in the choice of subject and its translation onto canvas. In *Ave Maria at Bolzano,* exhibited in 1857 at the British Institution, the artist has dramatically progressed from the sombre earlier works of the German hillsides. These betray a heaviness of treatment and perhaps an over-dramatization of the scene. In this grand work, the evening light pervades the setting of an outdoor celebration of Mass. This act of simple piety is represented by the group of peasants with their animals, collected around the priest. This painting, now in a private collection, indicates the artist's qualitative development over a short period of time. The artist has ceased to employ the darker earth colours of his palette, bringing this scene to life, with colour and warmth. Bridell now depicts immense vistas, a vastness and scope in the same mould as Turner. The evening light pervades the scene, reflecting small details, the shepherd bringing in his flock, the distant town nestled beside the lake. Details are not dissolved but highlighted to indicate the scale and depth of the scene. He is beginning to demonstrate how light works in nature and make it work in his pictures. Nor are some details accentuated at the expenses of others. They are incorporated with the balance that he senses is part of the whole setting, giving a sense of 'rightness' about the composition. Such is his technical mastery in passages of the painting, that the evening light, casting a bronzed glow, passes across the picture creating the contrasting light and the shadow. The light is used to dramatically emphasise the trees. In the evening shadow, the small group is almost tangibly subdued and quiet. In this scene, and further works from Northern Italy, the exercises of copying and recording of nature by the hitherto student is overtaken by the now developing ability of a craftsman.

This large work was the first likely introduction of James Henry Wolff to Bridell's work. Wolff, was to play an important part in Bridell's future and he went on to acquire the works the artist produced from sketches that had been made in Germany and Northern Italy. He recognised the future potential of the young artist although he was not a dealer or collector of art. In regard to *Ave Maria*, the transaction was likely to have been made by the artist with Wolff directly and thus provided the artist with an opportunity to discuss his future situation. It no doubt signalled the possibility for Bridell to establish a secure future away from the hitherto restricting hold of his employer.

It is however at the Liverpool Academy later that year, that Bridell aroused a great amount of interest with his *Sunset on the Atlantic*. This work excited admiration for its treatment of sea and sky and it was sold directly from the exhibition. The work has never since been seen publicly. In the same exhibition was a work by Edmund Havell Jnr. entitled *Rustic Scene, Lake Chiemsee, Bavaria*. The coincidence indicates that Havell and Bridell had worked in the same location in Bavaria, possibly at the same time, and indicates additional evidence for his link with the Havell family.

★ ★ ★

Queen Victoria and her husband, in both public and private lives, took a keen interest in art and artists. As was the practice amongst upper class Victorian ladies, she had a drawing tutor and produced her own watercolours. Privately she made visits to meetings of the Old Water Colour Society which were attended by William Havell, and other full members. She made private viewings of the Royal Academy exhibitions. The particular viewing of 1856 was attended by her seven children and Charles Eastlake. Lady Eastlake records how the smaller children hung onto her skirts and she admonished them saying 'Children, you are always in the way'.[39] Publicly, they attended the Royal Academy exhibitions each year. The royal couple frequently also sent out to have certain pictures 'of the moment' despatched to them on loan, from the gallery that they were being exhibited in. This possibly added to the publicity value of the work but caused some confusion in the galleries concerned. Nevertheless, Victoria and her husband kept abreast of the developments in the art world during this changeable period. It was the Prince Consort who was to promote an immense undertaking, that of the Royal Manchester Exhibition of 1857.

The exhibition comprised a total of almost 2,200 works of art of which over half were works of the Old Masters and seven hundred of the Modern Masters. There were also 386 British portraits. Eight weeks after the opening, the daily attendance figures were still averaging 9000. The Exhibition of 1851 had highlighted the achievement of industry, but this exhibition related the history of art in its best works, presenting the achievement of painters who were working at the time, alongside those of the Old Masters. This was the first major art exhibition in England and it was made possible by the generosity of the English collectors of the day. More importantly it removed the hitherto centre of the artworld from London and provided the industrial north with a prestigious event, to which the cultured middle-class would be drawn. The literary and influential figures of the day made particular arrangements to visit the exhibition.

It was at this time that the contract with Holder was providing Bridell with personal difficulties, which were likely to have been of a financial nature. It may have been the case that he was to justify his expenses from Holder against the number of sellable works. *The Dictionary of National Biography* in its article on Bridell amplifies the situation. The artist's time 'was being jealously accounted for and his work remaining mortgaged to his master.' It is probable that he instigated negotiation with Holder and in due course this became a very difficult period. The article suggests he endeavoured to buy himself out in 1857 and was unsuccessful. The article states that he finally bought himself out after he had married in 1860. Certainly the situation caused his health to fail and Henry Rose confirms this in his letter of Jan 1888. However, in contradiction to this view, a letter from his wife confirms that his health had revived before he started for Rome in the summer of 1858.[40]

Over this particular aspect of Bridell's life lies some uncertainty. There is also the fact that as an apprentice, Bridell would have needed Holder's permission to marry. In this case, it is unlikely that this was sought. The article mentioned, in suggesting that he bought himself out in 1859, appears to overlook the fact that the contract was due to be re-negotiated in any case at the end of the year. There is a strong case for the situation being resolved in 1857. The outcome was that Holder acquired a body of pictures, which were the product of his years in Bavaria.These, and cash, were the price Bridell had to pay in order to break away from the exploitation of his employer. His output from 1857 onward goes, by and large, to Mr.Wolff, his patron. Works after this date also appear not to be numbered, as they were previously and this suggests that on the acquisition of a studio, Bridell was freed from this onerous contract.

During this year he took up residence in Southampton at Highfield Lodge (illus). He was twenty six years of age. The acquisition of a studio was a landmark in his career and marked the rise in his fortune as an artist. He commemorated the event by a small oval work entitled

Temple of Vesta
Courtesy of Christies

In *My Atelier*, (also entitled *Scraps in an Atelier*).

He provided an interesting description of the subject of this work which reveals his careful choice of subject and an overriding sense of the influences that interested him at this time:

> "To the fanciful this work may be supposed to typify several periods of eventful history. The canvas with the saints's head drawn upon it in the early Italian manner of Perugino (master of Raphael) points to the 15th century; the document with the broad seal of England in the time of Henry V111. Attached to it, and the old vellum books, to the 16th century; the upright brown-backed book with Liber Veratatis upon it, to the 17th century; the minutely-pencilled leaf and fruit, and other still life, to the style of art most prevalent and best executed by the Flemings and the Dutch in the 18th century; and the hat of Tyrol of the kind they wear in the birthplace of Hofer, the champion of Tyrol, in the 19th century".
> Christies Sale Catalogue 27/02/1865

We can appreciate that Bridell continued in his own self-education and had triumphed over the limitations of his earlier upbringing. He also had a portrait taken (frontispiece) by an early method of photography, possibly an ambrotype or calotype.

Bridell was now free to set to work on an immense subject which had been 'lying dormant' in his imagination for some years. Very probably this work was based on *The Temple of Vesta*, which he had worked on seven years earlier. Inspired by the description of a setting in Spenser's *Faerie Queen*, he was to create a monumental work from the synthesis of the poem and his earlier work. It was to demonstrate the fullest expression of his capabilities and Bridell hoped it would be the realisation of a longheld ambition. From Henry Rose's letter, it is likely this was the work that Bridell hoped would one day hang between Claude and Turner in the National Gallery, thus demonstrating the artist's overriding conviction in his own ability. There is no doubt that he emulated Turner, but there is also a sense in which he rivalled him, as Turner had himself stood, in respect and rivalry to Claude.

This canvas was the largest work so far attempted by the artist, and measured 90x60 ins. It occupied Bridell for most of 1857 and early 1858 and had been commissioned by Wolff. This work and that of a study completed in 1859, now in the Southampton Art Gallery collection, is similar in subject, except for the number of figures in the foreground. In the 1850 painting, there is a group of nymphs. In the later painting, the group has been replaced by one solitary figure, seated in the near foreground.

Bridell's patron was James Henry Wolff. He was a shipping agent with offices in Canute Road. In partnership with a Mr Phillips, he imported goods from the South Americas, mainly tobacco and cigars. They may also have been instrumental in gaining for Southampton the prestigious contract of the Royal Mails from the packet ships, which had been previously handled by the port of Plymouth. Thus he helped to secure Southampton's future as a central point for foreign administration and communication.

By 1844 the Bevois Mount Estate had been divided up into lots for building and sold to a William Betts. He enlarged the house on the estate, adding lakes, fountains, greenhouses and arbours. The main gateway was enhanced with stone pillars surmounted by stags which gave its name to the junction of the Avenue and Lodge Road. James Wolff purchased part of the property and began a large collection of items relating to art and music in Bevois Mount House. The Bridell Gallery became a feature of the house and Mr Wolff commissioned the major works by Bridell over the following four years. He generously allowed interested parties to view this collection. Undoubtedly, over the next few years, Bridell was a regular visitor to the house.

The major work The *Temple of Vesta,* and the resulting payment was in effect Bridell's passport to the Continent. He was now free to pursue his own choice of subjects within the

Print from Turner's Italy.

37

requirements of his patron. At the beginning of September 1858, the artist set out for Rome. He travelled down the Rhine to Italy, spending some weeks in the vicinity of the Italian lakes. With the recent development of the railway system the journey could now be made directly between Coblenz, Basel and Lucerne, saving precious hours of travelling time.[41]

★ ★ ★

The possibility of continental travel for English travellers had been curtailed by the wars with France and the blockade imposed by Napoleon. Following his defeat in 1815, a new era had begun and travel on the continent was again possible. Importantly for artists there was the opportunity to study the art treasures that Napoleon had collected in the Louvre. Turner had filled notebooks with sketches from the works of Raphael, Correggio, Giorgione, Titian and Poussin. In the course of his campaigns Napoleon had made improvements to roads and transport. The first coaching roads over the Alps and the Route Napoleon along the west bank of the Rhine had been completed. The railway was also rapidly expanding, linking major town and cities, thus replacing the stagecoach services. But this development was fragmentary. Separate states in Italy, each with a distinct border, had no common co-ordinating body to implement these changes on a national scale.

The passion for travel was accompanied by travel diaries and literary travel memoirs of the most diverse type. We know that Bridell wrote descriptions of his travels in notebooks. A further genre which developed as a direct result of this pursuit were the travellers practical guidebooks, taking as their model John Murray's *Handbooks for Travellers*, published in 1842. Illustrated travel guides fuelled the demand for topographical engravings. In 1833 Samuel Prout's *Facsimiles of Sketches in Flanders and Germany* had appeared as a large book of lithographs which resembled an artist's portfolio of sketches. Ruskin and his father pored over this work and were consequently influenced to visit the sites of the illustrations. Turner himself, having begun his career as a topographical draughtsman, supplied many designs for engravings and profited considerably from this development. He completed twenty five vignettes for another successful and influential work of the time, Samuel Roger's poem *Italy*. The Brownings used this and Murray's popular handbook as a guidebook for their journeys in Italy. Samuel Prout (1783-1852), and J. D. Harding, amongst others, earned their living by providing drawings of continental towns and scenery for the same purpose. These appeared in *The Annuals,* which were comparatively cheap editions of landscape images. Such was the public enthusiasm for pictures of foreign lands that artists travelled great distances into uncharted territory. One, whose life is documented is W. H. Bartlett (1809-1854), a man who travelled thousands of miles, encountering unimaginable difficulties and retaining throughout, the manners and decorum of an Englishman. He was fortunate in his struggle to support his wife and children that he was almost constantly in demand for his work. During his short life, he had almost a thousand plates engraved from his drawings (see appendix).

In keeping with many Victorian writers and artists, Turner was a passionate traveller for whom encountering unfamiliar landscapes, cities, and people was a necessary stimulus. Fellow artists, Richard Wilson, Samuel Prout, William Havell, John Sell Cotman, Samuel Palmer, Clarkson Stanfield, David Roberts and Charles Eastlake, all made the journey to Rome. At every turn, there was the ever present reminder of history of a great civilisation.There was the inspiring quality of the light and as Eastlake describes, there was the added pleasure in the companionship of other artists.

'We go out as soon as it is light to paint and draw; then, at twelve, you see all the painters, true as the dial to the sun, returning – some from Mount Catillus, some from the villas of Maecenas, D'Este, the Temple of Venus, &c.,to dinner. If they are Germans or Italians they sleep an hour after; if French or English they are out again immediately until dark, when a supper is prepared, and when we English dine together; and, having a flute and a guitar among us, the labours of the day generally finish with the song and the waltz.'[42]

It was the publication by Lord Byron of his verse epic *Childe Harold's Pilgrimage* which had the greatest impact and inspired travel to the countries of our classical past. He incorporated his experiences into the third and fourth cantos of his 'pageant of the bleeding heart' which appeared in 1818. It was not intended as a guidebook, but became, in effect, the 'manual for a generation of tourists'. The secret of its power lay in its transfusion of landscape and history. Byron became famous overnight. The figure of Harold caught the imagination ; restless, torn, melancholy, passionate and ironic. A great many enthusiastic readers followed in the footsteps of the hero, amongst these was Turner who added quotations from the poem to his pictures. In 1841 he had completed a series of views of the fortress at Ehrenbreitstein, with the addition of Byron's lines from Manfred. Bridell also travelled with a copy of Byron's poem, which he read as he visited the same locations.

At each border crossing and along the principal roads, customs inspections were also necessary, a tiresome procedure which increased as the travellers went further south. Here there was the expectation of bribery of officials checking dutiable articles, who were readily paid in order not to delay the journey. We, now so familiar with foreign travel, can only imagine the agitation of this encounter with an alien culture. Besides the difficulties of conversing in Italian, 'which was not often attempted', there was for the foreigner, the experience of the rites and rituals of Catholicism and the Italian temperament. A particular incident related by the writer Nathaniel Hawthorne, provides an amusing anecdote, as he describes his family's departure from Rome.

> 'We left Rome this morning, after troubles of various kinds, and a dispute in the first place with Lalla, our female servant, and her mother....Mother and daughter exploded into a livid rage, and cursed us plentifully, wishing that we might never

come to our journey's end, and that we might all break our necks or die of apoplexy-the most awful curse that an Italian knows how to invoke upon his enemies, because it precludes the possibility of extreme unction. However, as we are heretics, and certain of damnation therefore anyhow, it does not much matter to us.'[43]

As to the travelling, Nathaniel Hawthorne records in his diaries 'Beggars indeed, started up at every point when we stopped for a moment and whenever a hill imposed a slower pace upon us'. Incidents, such as being left by the side of the road by the driver, or being threatened by robbers was not unknown.

Preparation for the journey, however carefully undertaken, was no guarantee against difficulties which could be encountered on the road. An incident in her memoirs, described by Lady Eastlake, furnishes a description of one of the trials for an unwary traveller.

> 'People say the Mt. Cenis pass has no scenery, but I fount it magnificent. The mountains are of the finest forms, loaded with snow above, clothed with woods below, and bright with the gayest of flowers to the top…..The posthouse was a little down the Italian side, and on changing horses we desired the new postilion to drive slowly. He answered 'Oui, oui j'irai doucement' and immediately set off with greater fury than the last, the consequence being that we felt a tremendous jolt, and found the tire of the wheel broken.
>
> We turned back to the posthouse where the postmaster, a fat old porpoise who could hardly breathe, but was determined to cheat us as long as he could, said he had no carriage to give us. We asked to look at his printed instructions, for we knew that these postmasters are bound to provide carriages for posting travelers; but he had no rules and said he had never heard of any such things. Ultimately he let us have what he said was his own carriage for three napoleons and gave us a receipt..'[44]

Elizabeth Browning records in 1859, the anticipated journey to Florence – the rapid way 'in which there are four hours of railway-and as we take a vettura with four horses, and six up the hills, we shall do it in four days.… And I dare say we shall not be confiscated by brigands, particularly as we travel in a large party, making up five men among us.'[45] On another occasion she describes a journey to Rome 'The most delightful journey we had from Florence-seven days of it. So strange it is, living on the road in that way. We had books in the carriage and I translated two or three German poems…'[46]

There were inevitably the added problems of bad roads and inclement weather. One of the major dangers of the journey was unavoidable, crossing the Alps. These difficulties were not

Rhine Sketches
Courtesy of Southampton Art Gallery

resolved until the St Gothhard rail tunnel opened in 1882.

★ ★ ★

Of Bridell's journey of 1858 we know that he spent some time in the vicinity of the Rhine, at the Fortress Enhrenbreitstein, completing later a large work 35x50 ins. of the scene. It was a format that he began to use increasingly from this period. A sheet of sketches from this time survives in Southampton Art Gallery. It shows a view of the Drachenfel mountains and boats on the river. The dates indicate his progress from Coblenz on 5th Sept. From here he continued to Basel with a change of train to Lucerne on the 7th September. He spent two weeks here before travelling on to Italy.

It is just possible that he visited Lausanne, approximately a hundred miles from Lucerne, and saw the works of the Swiss watercolour painter Ducros (1748-1810). Ducros had worked on large scale watercolours, and these were only available privately in England, at Stourhead in Dorset. Ducros had, in the tradition of Piranesi, completed an impressive rendering of the Coliseum, with the clever use of distorted perspective. But if we read

Bridell's description of how he came to decide on his particular viewpoint for the work, we are left in no doubt that he did not take the inspiration for the piece from another work. Ducros also tackled subjects of historical interest in Rome, which have some common elements in their treatment with that of Bridell. Ducros, whose work has been described as souvenir painting for Grand Tourists, took watercolour out of its accepted format. He emphasised the sublime and the monumental, and Turner was influenced by these works when he saw them at Stourhead. In effect the movement away from topographical representation towards a Romantic view is seen in Ducros' work. The landscape is seen as a link with the classical past but there is an increasing emphasis on the subjective experience of the artist.

From Lucerne, Bridell would have travelled by paddle steamer to Fluelen. Thereafter the journey was by the mail coach over the St Gotthard Pass. A perilous journey if undertaken in winter but a breathtaking experience at the height of summer. He arrived at Camerlata near Como by the 22nd. He spent some few weeks in the area, before a brief visit to Venice and arrived in Rome in early November. He found himself a studio on the Pincian Hill, in the Via Gregoriana. It was situated on the fourth floor of the building and commanded a view over the city, from the rear. His lodging was taken in an adjoining Street, at 72 Via Sistina. The location was within a short distance from the studio in Piazza Mignanelli, which had been occupied by Eastlake and where Turner had painted on his visit in 1829.

In December, he writes to his patron, James Wolff:
Rome 2/12/58.

"I am now settled as far as the studio is concerned most capitally on the Pincian Hill overlooking Rome – the best lighted, most healthy and most agreeable quarter (in dirty Rome) possibly to be selected.

I have been nearly a month here now, and have begun painting your second large picture. After partially completing many large subjects from the sketches I made in my journey hither, of which I have a great number, and some very capable of producing beautiful pictures, I have at last decided upon one of the grandest themes I believe possible for a landscape painter to select. I should like to tell you how I first came to think of it. After coming from the Academy, (to which I immediately attached myself upon arriving here) about 10 o'clock one fine night, I went along to the end of the Corso and as you leave it (the fashionable quarter of Rome) the whole appearance and atmosphere of the place changed. Traversing some filthy streets of Old Rome which commence here you emerge, all suddenly upon the ruins of a temple – very vast, but almost effaced-pass it and then another, and yet another and you come to the Forum – in itself a whole heap of debris of temples and palaces, with the Capitol looking down solemnly upon it. Go through the grand arch of the Temple of Peace, across its floor and then standing underneath the shadow of the Temple of Venus and looking south, there rises gigantically and almost oppressively before you the old gladiators' circus – The Coliseum. Accident caused my first visit to it by a starry and beautiful night; but all who wish freely to enjoy its immensity and solemn beauty should scrupulously avoid seeing it first by daylight. I immediately came to my present decision regarding your picture.

The next night I took two men (cut-throat looking blackguards they were to be sure) together with lamps, easel, canvas &c and painted there on the spot till about 2 o'clock in the morning when the moon began to decline and the constellation of Orion appeared in the sky with everything absolutely still. The whole was very perfect, very solemn and most impressive. I read over Byron's fine description of the Coliseum in Manfred whilst looking at the thing itself.

> "The gladiator's bloody circus stands
> A noble wreck, in ruinous perfection,
> While Caesar's chambers, and the Augustand halls
> Grovel on earth, in distinct decay."

The Academy referred to in the letter was the Academy of St. Luke which is described by Hawthorne as the Fine Arts Academy at Rome. It was located in the via Bonella, which was close to the Forum. In the collection 'which was not vastly large, but the pictures were in more presentable condition than usual', were works by Van Dyck, Veronese, several by Titian, two or more by Guido. In the gallery there were rows of portraits of members of the Academy, most of whom, he observes, 'judging by their physiognomies, were very commonplace people'.[47] Bridell also copied works in the Villa Borghese and those by Poussin and Claude in the Farnese Palace. Hawthorne describes these treasures in his writings and he describes how he was particularly drawn to works by Guido, believing that …'Guido has made the sun to rise as no landscapist –no Claude even, nor Turner has done'.

The sights and sounds of Rome also gave rise to poetic description in journals and letters. More than any other building the Coloseum provoked strong emotions. This monumental edifice is impressive today, how more so it was then, with the fallen decoration surrounding its base and the public traffic consisting of horses and carts. It was fashionable to visit the ruin by moonlight and imagine the ghosts of its past which may have haunted the darker recesses. Lady Eastlake's journal gives us her impressions which arose from visiting the Coloseum. She betrays the ambiguous response to this great achievement of an ancient empire which had exercised incomprehensible brutality in the pursuit of entertainment.

'Yesterday morning we drove to the Coliseum, turning off through more remote parts of the city, wretched and filthy as the worst parts of the old town of Edinburgh. Soon traces of a race of giants began to appear – masses of masonry stamped with grandeur, fragments of columns – things I had always known though never realised before. Then came to the Capitol, the columns of the Temple of Concord, the triumphal arches – some whose feet lay deep buried in the earth, others which stood cleared in pits below the road. Then grand forms and colours, and the Temple of Peace, making one breathless with excitement. At last we saw, through other objects of ineffable grandeur, the great circle of the Coliseum. We drove under the Arch of Titus (this seemed profanation) past the remains of a fountain, where, the coachman said, the Romans washed their hands from the blood of the martyrs. It might be true, it might be false – but the few words filled to overflowing the mingled feelings which oppressed me, and, as we slowly approached the tremendous pile, my tears were falling. I got down and entered its vast precincts with awe – the martyrs much in my thoughts, but also that noble race, so great, selfish, wise and cruel, which did all man can do without revelation. It was in utter solitude, an old world of itself, dedicated to the worst passions of humanity, and yet the triumph and exponent of almost Godlike power. The blue sky shone through the bare spaces of the windows, bluer than you can conceive, thus enframed within the glowing colours of these sunny piles, as blue to me as it had been for ages to them; and as I looked around at all the grand adaptation of means to an end, and at the overpowering majesty and beauty which were the result, I felt proud that my nation was more truly the descendant of that matchless race than of any other in the world. Indeed I felt that I belonged to both the Christian martyr and the Roman decemvir, and perhaps I pitied and admire, the last as much as I did the first…'[48]

Rome was the magnet which drew artists and sculptors of all nationalities to live and work closely together. A small group of German artists, the Nazarenes, were working there at this time. They had formed a brotherhood under the guidance of Overbeck, and sought to unite the purity of art with the primacy of religion. Of the American artists in Rome at the time was William Story, who has left a record of his experiences here. He was a sculptor in Rome and was also a great friend of Robert Browning, Mrs Gaskell and Nathaniel Hawthorne.

Nathaniel Hawthorne had been employed as consul in Liverpool since 1853 and had moved to Rome in early 1858 with his wife and two children. Here they remained for eighteen months as he worked on the book *The Marble Faun*. They took a keen interest in art throughout their travels, and both sketched when the opportunity arose. His *Notebooks* and also those of his wife provide us with an interesting and sometimes amusing account of life in Rome, contemporaneous with Bridell's stay. He eloquently describes the atmosphere of Rome at this period and provides us with vivid descriptions of the daily sights that Bridell also saw. He and his family resided in apartments in an area close to Bridell's studio.

Palazzo Larazani Via Porta Pinciana

'Cold, narrow lanes, between tall, ugly, mean-looking, whitewashed houses, sour bread, pavements most uncomfortable to the feet, enormous prices for poor living; beggars, pick-pockets; ancient temples and broken monuments, and clothes hanging to dry about them, French soldiers, monks and priests of every degree; a shabby population, smoking bad cigars – these would have been some of the points of my description. Of course there are truer and better things to be said........'[49]

His wife records her first impression in her diary of 14/2/1858:

'We have been in Rome since 20th January and have not written a word of my journal.

Till the 2nd it was bitterly cold and afterward but little milder, and not sufficiently so to make my fingers flexible enough to hold a pen. On the 5th it began to rain, the weather previously having been clear and brilliant. The rain softened the air, or it rained because the air was softer and rained on till the 12th. Now again it is glorious sunshine and cold; but everyone says the winter has gone....I have walked about and seen glimpses of what is before me. I have walked through the Forum Romanum and seen the Arch of Septimus Severus, the portico of the Temple of Saturn, the three beautiful columns of the Temple of Minerva Chalcidica, the single column erected to the Emperor Phocas.. terminated by the Arch of Titus.'[50]

These landmarks, in becoming so familiar to Bridell, provided the inspiration that was to spur him on to completing large works of these impressive ruins.

Elizabeth and Robert Browning were also resident in Rome at this time. They usually spent the winter in Rome and then returned north to Florence or Siena, for the summer. They resided in a crowded, less airy part of the town, less than half a mile from the Pincian Hill. They were spending the winter here on account of Elizabeth's health. Regarded as the greatest woman poet of the time, she was a passionate but frail individual. Mrs Hawthorne records a striking description of her when she visited her in Florence.

'At one o'clock I took U & R (her abbreviations for her children) to Casa Guidi to see Mrs Browning. She does not see people till eight in the evening; but as R is fast asleep at that hour, she requested me to come at one with her. We rang a great while, and no one answered the bell, but presently a woman came up the staircase and admitted us; but she was surprised that we expected to see Mrs Browning at such a time. I gave her my credentials and so she invited us to follow her in.

We found the wondrous lady in her drawing room, very pale and looking ill yet she received us affectionately and was deeply interesting as usual. She took R into her lap and seemed to enjoy talking to and looking at her, as well as U. She said 'Oh, how rich and happy you are to have two daughters, a son and such a husband'. Her boy was gone to his music masters which I am very sorry for, but we saw a picture of him. Mrs Browning said he had a vocation for music but did not like to apply to anything else more than a butterfly and the only way she could command his attention was to have him upon her knees and hold his hands and feet. He knows German pretty well already and Italian perfectly being born a Florentine.

I was afraid to stay too long or to have Mrs Browning talk because she looked so pale and seemed so much exhausted, and I perceived that the motions of R's fan distressed her. I do not understand how she can live long, or be at all restored while she does live.

I ought to say that she lives so ardently that her delicate earthly vesture must soon be burnt up and destroyed by her soul of pure fire'.[51]

Elizabeth doted on her son Weideman whom she called Peni, or sometimes Penini. As she had suffered several miscarriages, he was the focus of her existence. He is recorded as a tense little boy, taking life as seriously and as emotionally as his mother. Both of them revered Louis Napoleon. 'Now we Italians (such as Pen and I) …' She did not approve of the British political stance by Lord Derby, believing in Napoleon as 'the agent for a free Italy'. Her disappointment over England's reluctance to engage in the struggle is given expression in her *Songs Before Congress* of 1860. By her marriage to Robert Browning, she had severed the strong family tie with her father. He had, by this date died without a reconciliation between them. There was no legacy left to the daughter who had once been his favourite child. Fortunately their modest wants were catered for due to her benefactor, a Mr Kenyon. In speaking of her work, she declares…' I have worked at poetry – it has not been with me reverie, but art… Poetry has been as serious a thing to me as life itself; and life has been a very serious thing; there has been no playing at skittles for me in either.'[52]

Elizabeth Browning, writing regularly to her family, provides us with much of the social background to their lives in Italy. It is in a letter to Arabella her sister, in February 1859 that she describes a social occasion. For her and her husband, it was a small social gathering. But for Bridell and Eliza Florance Fox, it was an event of great importance, their marrriage. In the letter, we discover that the artist had visited the Brownings in Rome on several occasions. He had known his intended bride only a matter of a few months. The couple had met earlier in 1858 in London, as Eliza later records. Bridell had not met members of her family, but rather than delay matters and return to England, they made their vows in Rome. The wedding was a

Elizabeth Barrett-Browning

quiet and simple affair. It may not have entirely been coincidental that she happened to meet him in Rome at the latter part of the year. There is a hint from one source, that this headstrong and capable woman had 'followed' him to Italy.

The Brownings had ten rooms of varying sizes, none of them very big, but the sitting room was adequate to accommodate themselves and at least 13 named guests. It was used early in 1859 for a smaller more intimate affair.

'We have had a wedding here' writes Elizabeth to Arabella, 'and Robert has "given away" the bride, who is no other than Miss Fox. She came out here this winter for purposes of art & chose to begin my portrait, as I think I told you,- and fell in with Mr.Bridell a landscape-painter of much talent who brought letters to us in Florence & whom we have seen a little since. A week ago the two arrived in company to pay me a morning visit – Said Bridell, "Miss Fox has something to say to you, Mrs Browning – Had I better go out of the room?"..to Miss Fox. I exclaimed…."You frighten me – what is it?" Before I had settled into a decided

47

tremble, came the information from the male visitor...." The fact is, we are thinking of being TIED, & it would be a great gratification to both of us if you would consent to be witnesses." – Such a surprise! So Robert went as witness, & I should have done the same if a cold wind had not forbidden it –To make up for which omission bride & bridegroom & bride's cousin were invited to dinner the same day with us. Do you think they came? Yes, most willingly. We dined at six, had champagne & everything in order, & our visitors remained till half past ten- Seldom in the course of my life have I been so tired to death – And they...you would think the bride had done nothing else but be married every day. An extraordinary serenity of mind & spirits for the occasion, certainly. Immediately after the ceremony they went to the Corso (where the carnival is carried on) then to dinner (with us) at six. This was on Saturday: on Monday they were at their respective studios as usual. Mr. Fox had written from England to entreat Robert to take his place at the ceremony – and so, went. Then she is an energetic little creature, to whom I wish well – and really have proved my goodwill by submitting to be "sacrificata" in sitting for my portrait......'[53]

The marriage had taken place at the British Consulate Office in Rome on February 26 1859. Eliza Florance Fox, was some six years older than her husband. The marriage certificate is witnessed by an Emily Friell, a friend of Eliza, George E.Fox, Eliza Fox's cousin and travelling companion, and Robert Browning. The occupation of Bridell's father is given as 'builder' and that of his bride's father, as 'Member of Parliament'.

Of those who knew Eliza well, we have a little description by Mrs Gaskell, just after she had met Charlotte Bronte in 1850. She records the following comparison. 'Miss Bronte is a nice person. Like you, Tottie, but without your merriment: poor thing she can hardly smile. She has led such a hard, cruel (if one may dare to say so) life. She is quite sensible, unaffected, with high, noble aims.'[54] Another description of Eliza says 'she had a lovely expressive dark face, such eyes, and a low broad Grecian brow.'[55]

Eliza had communicated regularly, for the previous ten years, with Mrs Gaskell. She had visited the family in Cheshire and was often consulted regarding the education of her daughters). Mrs Gaskell had published *Mary Barton* in 1848 which had made a deep impression on Victorian Society.) When Mrs Gaskell learned that Eliza was to visit Rome with her cousin George in the summer of 1858, she was rather taken by surprise at the hastily arranged trip. 'I think I can give you some nice introductions in Rome, and to George too... but not to Monsignors (I only know one) or Cardinals...But you and George should know our dear Mr Story, who would know what you should do, and Mr Page, the American artist.'[56]

Mrs Gaskell was overwhelmed to read of Eliza's sudden marriage in *The London Times*. Just the minimum of three lines in the Marriage column recorded that the event had taken place. She had had no inkling of the affair and wrote an impassioned letter to William Fox, demanding the details.

42 Plymouth Grove
Manchester
March 10th 1859

My dear Mr Fox,

Our Times of today – well of yesterday-well, tomorrow it will be of some day in dream land, for I am past power of counting-

Our Times of today has taken away my breath-Who-What, Where, Wherefore,Why – oh! do be a woman, and give me all possible details- Never mind the House of Commons: it can keep – but my, our, curiosity CAN'T–

Oh! please telegraph back anything about him – how long known what is he – what has he (I live in Manchester city sacred to Mammon,) when did she first see him— Where are they going live– Whole love story, &c., &c.,&c.

Write for 26 hours consecutively, and you can't write enough.

WELL TO BE SURE
I THINK I AM
VERY
GLAD.

Yours most truly
E.C.Gaskell

Subsequently, from Mrs Gaskell, we learn that the couple are now residing in the Piazza Barberini. She writes to Eliza (sic) on March 21st, their letters having crossed in the post.

'You are a good darling, for remembering to write to me, and tell me all about it. It does sound very nice. Fancy your meeting your fate at Rome.(I dreamt of you and your husband at Albano, in the gardens of the Villa Medici – think of me if you go there). I want to know a quantity more of course. Where were you lodging first in Rome? What were you married in? Roman scarves and cameos? Oh, and is not Rome above every place you imagined? And do you go to the Pamphile Doria villa, and gather anemonies,….. and do you know the Storeys, and have you seen Mr. Page? Where are you going to when Rome gets unhealthy, if you are going to stay till August in Italy. And how come the Brownings in Rome? Will you give my very kindest regards to her, and my kind regards to him….and can you bring me back anything from Rome that is not very large and handsome, or will it plague you, and the unknown man, who after all will look after your luggage, and must therefore be consulted. But I like the 'sound' of him

49

extremely, and I hope he will like me when we come to know each other, which must not be long first.'[57]

Mrs Gaskell, followed this letter, with one to her daughter Marianne in late March, in which she refers to the letter from Eliza… 'One from Tottie, which I am sorry to say I lost as soon as read, or you should have seen it. She describes her husband as very charming, & seems very happy. ….they come home in August; have rooms in the Piazza Barberini'. Further short notes, cited later, indicate that Mrs Gaskell continued to visit the couple on their return to England.[58]

The friendship between Robert Browning and William Johnson Fox, Eliza Fox's father, was longstanding. Fox's own life story from impoverished beginnings to Member of Parliament provides interesting background to the struggles of the working class (see Appendix). We read in Elizabeth Browning's letter dated 30/8/55 that …'Tomorrow evening however we go to meet Frederick Tennyson; and last night she, (Mrs Sartoris) the Tennysons, Mr Forster and Mr Fox spent the evening with us.' Robert Browning continued to acknowledge his gratitude and friendship towards Fox in his letters to him.[59]

Fox's recognition of genius was fortuitous for the young Robert Browning. His earliest poem, *Pauline* appeared in the *Monthly Repository* in April 1833. Fox was immediately impressed by the work and wrote in praise of its author 'these thoughts have been suggested by the work before us, which, though evidently a hasty and imperfect sketch, has truth and life in it, which gave us the thrill, and laid hold of us with the power, the sensation of which has never yet failed us as a test of genius.' Fox's recognition of genius was fortuitous for the young Robert Browning. Fox wrote, 'We cannot judge of the house by the brick, but we can judge of the statue of Hercules by its foot. We felt certain of Tennyson, before we saw the book, by a few verses which had straggled into a newspaper; we are not less certain of the author of *Pauline*.[60] Subsequent editions, saw the first publications of Browning's works until 1841.

Eliza Fox recalls in the same article, a visit by Browning to her home. 'I see myself, a child, sitting drawing at a sunny cottage window in the then rural suberb of Bayswater. Puffs of sweet scents of hawthorn and roses came floating in at the open window as I drew.' On learning that William Fox was out and only Eliza at home, Browning entered the drawing room. "It's my birthday today; I'll wait until they come in", and sitting down at the piano, he added "If it won't disturb you, I'll play till they do". She remembers Browning as 'slim and dark, and very handsome; and — may I hint it — just a trifle of a dandy, addicted to lemon-coloured kid gloves and such things: quite 'the class of fashion and the mould of form. Full of ambition, eager for success, and what's more, determined to conquer fame and to achieve success'.

The political struggle which followed the Anti Corn Laws, was also one which attracted

Portrait of Edwin Holder. 1850. In private collection.

I

Detail Neapolitan Landscape. Bridell
Courtesy of Reading Art Gallery

The Plains of Sorrento. Engraved from painting by William Havell

II

The Val St.Nicola. J.D.Harding

Ave Maria at Bolzano.-detail
Courtesy of the owner

IV

The Coliseum by Moonlight
In private collection. Bridgeman Library

The Olive Groves at Varenna
In private collection

VI

Pine Trees at Castel Fusano

The Olive Groves at Varenna – detail

Bridell residences

Highfield Lodge,
Southampton

Entrance to 13 Via
Gregoriana, Rome

Houses at Sussex Place,
London

VIII

another leading industrialist of similar character to Fox. This was John Platt, for many years the owner of the engineering company Messrs. Platt Bros & Co. in Oldham. He had received only local schooling but took the greatest of interest in local and national politics. As Mayor for Oldham in 1861 he had worked tirelessly to improve the water supply and accommodation in the town. In 1865 and 1868 he was elected as Member of Parliament for Oldham. John Platt had married the only daughter of another factory owner Samuel Radcliffe. Radcliffe was elected as Mayor of St James Ward in Oldham on four occasions. Both families were closely linked and they owned large residences in Werneth Park, Oldham. Both Platt and Radcliffe were patrons of Bridell, and of the pictures submitted to the 1887 Exhibition at Manchester, two were then owned by Mrs S. R. Platt.

★ ★ ★

Eliza Fox and Barbara Leigh Smith, later Bodichon, were the first women artists to have their own exhibitions in London, at Mr Gambart's French Gallery (see Appendix). One of the leading writers of the day who visited these exhibitions as a matter of course was George Eliot, who was a good friend of Barbara Leigh Smith. She took a keen interest in art, visiting studios and exhibitions in London and when she travelled on the continent, recording impressions of these in her diaries and letters.

In 1857 The Society of Female Artists held their first exhibitions and Eliza Fox exhibited here almost every year for the following thirty years. She also exhibited at the Royal Academy from 1859 until 1871, the first picture was a portrait of her husband. Until 1859, Eliza Fox had regularly exhibited at Suffolk Street since 1846. She was most drawn to portraits, but she also worked at imaginative and genre subjects. She appears to have had little interest in landscape but there is one indication of a joint venture in Italy. A picture, at auction[61] in 2003 had an interesting inscription. The work was oil on paper 24x44.5 cms. In the sale catalogue it was described as follows: 'Coastal scene probably in the Mediterranean'. The inscription on the back read 'copy from F.Lee Bridell/by EFB'. It is possible that the work was completed during a trip from Rome, and they may have visited Sicily.

Throughout the early months of 1859, the artist was working on *The Coliseum*. A work which is in the tradition of poetical landscape, but combines drama, history, the passing moment and death. The painting so eloquently portrays these aspects to combine thought and feeling into a harmonious resolution of awe. The impressive edifice is a dark, gaunt shape against the prevailing moonlight. A group of barefoot Capuchins, bearing torches, head a dim funeral procession which steals along in the deep shadows. The movement of the monks and their torches, dwarfed in comparison with the magnificent building is again part of the grander theme of time and decay. There is a boldness in the conception and execution which is exhilarating. The artist has transformed the scene by the precise fixing of the clouds against the moon, which heightens the work's dramatic impact, creating a silent and eerie spectacle.

Wolff had further commissioned a pair of large pictures to illustrate a classical theme in the setting of the Italian landscape. In this pursuit Bridell visited some of the lesser known areas away from Rome, as well as those more popular with the increasing numbers of tourists. In the event, he decided on the pine forest at Castel Fusano, an area of natural parkland north of Rome which bordered the coastline. Sending no works for exhibition himself, his wife submitted a portrait of her husband to the Royal Academy.

Returning to England, the couple resided for a time with Eliza's father in 3 Sussex Place, near Regent's Park. We know that Bridell had impressed Elizabeth Barrett Browning and she was eager to do what she could for the young artist. She proposed a meeting with her friend, John Ruskin. Mrs. Browning sent the following note to "John Ruskin Esq. Junior. Denmark Hill"[62]

> Mr Dear Mr. Ruskin
>
> I am writing to you but not today. This time it is simply to introduce to you, Mr Bridell, a very clever landscape painter, married here in Rome to the daughter of my husband's old friend Mr Fox of Oldham, who, she also, is devoted to art – for art's sake, therefore, & ours, will you suffer them to take your hand?
>
> Rome May 1

They also visited Eliza's brother, Franklin, who at this time owned a farm near Dorking. Some ten years younger than Eliza, he had been for most of his life, a master mariner in the Royal Navy. Evidently he gave some sketches to Bridell, who later worked on them and produced a work entitled *Whaling off Desolation Island*.

Exhibiting at the British Institution in February, he submitted the recently completed pair of pictures for Wolff's collection. *The Grotto of Neptune* (72 x 49 ins.) at Tivoli and *Pine Trees, Castel Fusano* (72 x 49 ins.). The review in the Art Journal is eloquent and assesses the work in characteristic terms.

'The upright form of this picture has enabled the artist to give not only the grotto, but also the fall above it. The whole is rendered with impressive truth; the treatment of the subject elevates it to a passage of grandeur, everywhere fully sustained by well-ordered dispositions. We are here also near the Grotto of the sirens and innumerable sites hallowed to the classic reader.'[63] He also exhibited a smaller work entitled *Tombs of the Scipios* which was described as a 'small and sparkling work, elegant in feeling'.

We learn from a note from Mrs Gaskell to her daughter Marianne, dated late Feb.1860 that her daughter ' Meta has gone to A.A.J's and I am to meet her at the Bridell's at half past three. If she and I have the time after the Bridell's, we shall go and call on Lady Verney, who is in town'.[64] A later letter on May 9th, is a short note to Eliza to warn her that she intends to make a visit 'before many days elapse'.[65] This was a happy time for Bridell and his wife and they were both doing well. He was now receiving the income from the sales of his pictures, and both painters were working hard on their art, interposed with parties and other hospitable occasions.[66] Here, or what is more probable, in a rented studio, husband and wife continued with their demanding schedule.

In May, *The Coliseum* was exhibited at the Royal Academy. In its conception it stood out against any other depiction of the Coliseum, overshadowing a smaller work exhibited by David Roberts. It received highly glowing reviews in *The Times* of 5th May.

> '.....but this like so many striking works of young men in the exhibition is a study not a picture, here are only the materials of pictures. The digesting of them into wholes is a further process which most of our young painters have yet to begin. Even Mr. Oakes (J.Wright Oakes) works such as 'The Bend of the River' and the 'Aberffian Bay' beautiful as they are in sky and foreground lack something of that completeness of balance and hue which goes to the making of a picture. Not so with Mr Bridell's *Moonlight view of the Coliseum*. Here the painter has selected one of the most impressive aspects of one of the most impressive of ancient remains – an aspect imaginatively harmonized with the ruin – and has represented it with a power and courage alike worthy of the subject. This picture at once gives Mr. Bridell high rank among our landscape painters.'

The Art Journal had begun life in 1839 and became a leading publication which created a following and an interest in the art of the day.(In style and content it is an invaluable reference to the Victorian art scene). In its review of the exhibition it also echoes the perceptions from *The Times* review of 1861.

> 'A felicitous conception is that of the Coliseum by moonlight; grand as the ruin is, it looks comparatively lame by day. It is presented here in its imposing magnitude, all detail lost and telling against the moonlight sky. The faithful shade betrays no other masses, shrinking as they do by daylight into mean proportion in this imposing presence. But in the light as in the shade, there is poetry; the sky is conceived in a spirit well fitted to accompany such a monument.'[67]

Two smaller studies were also made for this work.One of these, (size 31x45ins) was sold at Sothebys 7/6/1995 (l.46) and made £8625. Another work entitled *View of the Coloseum Rome*

(32 x 34.5 ins.), appeared in the Plint sale of 8/3/1862. The original sketch, done by moonlight, and of a very provisional nature, was kept by Bridell's wife until her death and later donated to Reading Art Gallery. So popular was the final painting that the *Illustrated London News* produced a full page engraving of the work in its July 28th edition.

Dr. Sweetman declares this work to be 'exceptional in scope and density. It transforms his achievement and demands a reassessment of his potentialities. It was the culmination of a decade of intense activity during which his style had rapidly changed'.[68]

★ ★ ★

For Bridell, this was undoubtedly a very settled and productive period. He had a patron, his wife had independent means and he was free from financial concerns. On the threshold of receiving the acclaim due to him and confident that wider recognition would soon be in his grasp, the couple were eager to return to Italy. The artist was to work on another pair of impressive subjects, again commissioned by Wolff. These were to be almost the same size as the large, recently executed work and to 'contain a sense of the historical past' in a landscape setting.

Approximately sixty kilometres north of Rome, on the Flaminian Way, Bridell began sketches in preparation for a large work entitled *Etruscan Tombs, Civita Castellana* (74 x 47 ins.), and it was to be a sunset scene. He may have seen works or sketches produced by Harding from his visit here in 1830. This work has not been traced, appearing at auction once in 1864, at the Bridell Gallery sale. It may well contain elements of the study in the possession of Southampton Art Gallery *Quarry Civita Castellana*. Bridell wrote his own description of the subject, to Wolff, and quoted a passage from a book which accompanied his travels, *Cities and Sepulchres of Etrusca*. Bridell's description was included in the sale catalogue of 1864.

> 'According to Denys and Gray, Cities and Sepulchres of Etrusca,' it is the supposed site of the ancient Falerii, an Etruscan city of great magnificence when Rome itself was but a village....The mountain that appears over the glen is Monte Soracte. The inscription over the tomb is 'Puripu' a name of one of the Lares or Penates (household deities). This inscription, 3,000 years old perhaps, still exists.'

For the second work, Bridell returned to another favourite spot of artists in Rome, that of Tivoli, and depicted the *Villa D'Este*. He exhibited *The Villa D'Este, Tivoli* and *The Woods of Sweet Chestnut above Varenna* at the British Institution for the following year (1861) This latter work was donated to the Tate Gallery by Mrs. Bridell-Fox, following the artist's death. With these paintings, he attracted a glowing tribute in *The Times* of Feb 11 for that year.

'Such strength as the exhibition has is in landscape.

In this class, besides a great number of unpretending little pictures-most of them representing with unimaginative literalness, the commonest aspects of rural and seaside English nature – we may point attention to a few canvases, conspicuous for higher aims or rarer qualities. First should be noticed Mr Bridell's two large Italian subjects, the *Villa D'Este, Tivoli* (62), and the *'Chestnut Woods above Varenna, Como* (244). The first shows us in the middle distance the noble group of cypresses in the villa garden, with a foreground of broad terrace and stately fountain-basin, and a wide outlook over the Alban plain under a glowing sun. On the left, in shadow, is the vast garden front of the villa. The foreground architecture and foliage are massively and powerfully painted. There is however, a want of glow and transparency in the aerial effects. Such a sun in such a sky should have flooded the distance with a serener splendour, and have given more sharpness and power to the foreground lights and shadows. Still, the picture is a large manly effort, and deserves particular recognition in the days of minute making out and multiplication of small detail.[69]

Mr Bridell's second picture is better still. The hour is close on evening. The gaunt and shattered chestnut wood stretches down the long sloping hill, which slants athwart the picture to the darkling blue of the lake; and over its broad shoulder is the deep lapis-lazuli blue of the evening sky, toning into a greenish hue as it nears the horizon on the left. The grandeur and solemnity of Italian landscape in its more sombre moments have been deeply felt and powerfully rendered by the painter, and there is poetry in his picture.'

A large work from this period, entitled *Temples at Agrigento* (58 x 40 ins), which has appeared once at auction,[70] the only occasion following the Bridell Gallery sale, is more problematical. There are no records of studies or sketches for this work or sketches completed in the locality. The Temples are in Sicily, and it is conceivable that Bridell travelled there on a very short visit. He may have worked on this view from sketches and looked at engravings that depicted this important site.

The Villa D'Este was the last painting by Bridell to go to the Bridell Gallery. Why this was so is a matter of conjecture. Perhaps Wolff was experiencing financial difficulties and it appears that he was not purchasing works from other hands.

For a struggling artist, a dealer was now the usual means off getting works seen by a wider public. Up to this time, only a handful of Bridell's pictures had been seen publicly. It was the influence of the dealer that was a chief characteristic of the years between 1850 and 1870. They had taken over the role of the patrons and due to their efforts were responsible for the immense increase in the prices of modern pictures. For a successful artist, such as Frith, as described in her memoirs by his daughter, the dealer was a welcome figure in these changing fortunes.

'In our day the picture dealer took the sordid bargaining out of Papa's hands save and except when he was inundated with commissions from enthusiastic admirers who implored him for more pictures than he could ever hope to paint.'[71]

One dealer in particular, Ernest Gambart, played an influential role in these changing times. Frith's daughter provides a sketch of this enterprising and influential man.

'Mr Gambart was a small, thin, and energetic Frenchman (Belgian), married to a charming wife, who used to have the most wonderful Sunday parties at a big house in St.John's Wood. In the summer it was his custom to take an equally large house and much bigger garden in the country, close to Stoke Poges, and here the parties became enormous, and we were given vast luncheons and teas in a great tent on the lawn.'[72]

The Art Journal saw its task as exposing the unscrupulous tactics, which had very often resulted in other dealers generally acquiring dubious reputations, as if they were all tarred with the same brush. The editor comments on art-dealers, almost as a self-appointed arbitrator. 'The "trade" in pictures is not only legitimate but very beneficial, there can be no doubt. Although we have done much to expose the tricks of dishonest deatlers, we have as earnestly sought to uphold those whose transactions are reasonable and upright: such unquestionably is Mr. Morby, who has long been known as a just dealer'. Bridell was fortunate in that he dealt with Joseph Morby, who had a gallery at Cornhill.

Returning to Italy in 1860 Bridell completed sketches for a monumental work, which was to be the same size as *The Temple of Vesta*, entitled *The Olive Groves at Varenna*. He spent several months at Lake Como, completing works at Abbadio Lariana, Menaggio and Cadennabia. This sojourn was also a tour, visiting the other lakes, Lecco and Lugarno. James Duffield Harding was also working in the area of Lucerne, at Brunnen, at the time, and it is interesting speculation that the artists met and discussed their work.

Lady Eastlake had recorded in her letter of 1854, her first impression of arriving at Varenna:

'...we made our way to Varenna, a place whose beauty nothing could conceal. There I had my first view of olive trees, which grow in the greatest richness on the south shores. The olive is a beautiful tree – so sharp when seen in its chiselled leaves against the sky, and so soft in it blue green mass in the distance'.[73]

This magnificent work (89x60 ins.) with the glow of afternoon light, brings the experience of Italy to life. In its unhurried pace of a late afternoon, the peasants take a rest at the well. It is an idyllic setting and one which the artist himself experienced. It is not a scene of the imagination, it has no echoes of the drama of previous works. Bridell has moved away from the preoccupations of his youth. This is the mature artist conveying the truth of the scene to us, with clarity and richness of colour. We can feel the sun spreading its warmth across the hillside. In effect it is a simple celebration of life and landscape. He was also working on several versions of *Woods of Sweet Chestnut* in this vicinity. In his love of trees and their representation he excelled, constantly interpreting the theme with confidence and competence.

Upon returning to England, the couple took up residence in Sussex Place, with William Fox. From here Bridell exhibited at the British Institution *Tremezza Mountains Menaggio*, and *Scene, Fiume Latte, Lake Lecco*. *The Times* review of the exhibition is of particular note as it focuses on the strength of Bridell's work, and aptly details his achievement. The reviewer mentions another popular artist, J.Wright Oakes, and his work *Camber Castle*, 1861:

> 'This is as beautiful a little picture as could be produced of a subject with no more prominent features than level marsh pasture, sweeps of yellow sand, and a low margin of sea, studded with monotonous martello towers.
>
> It would be difficult to find a better contrast between the ambitious and the unpretending in treatment and subject than is presented by this picture and Mr F.Lee Bridell's View on Como from Varenna, as you look across to Menaggio, clinging to the narrow strip of strand between the lake and the Tremezza mountains. This is a grand subject and Mr Bridell has treated it with a bold and manly pencil. It is refreshing to see work in which the strength and solidity of nature have evidently been felt and grappled with, as well as her colour and sunshine. If Mr Bridell could render the light of the sky as well as he models the forms of its clouds, and could concentrate his effect as powerfully as he can draw the lines of that magnificent Italian lake scenery, his work would leave little to desire. As it is, it deserves to be cited for strength and manliness, and a wise scorn of that pettiness and prettiness which threaten to be landscape painters to boulders and beck-sides, and to condemn them for ever to hard labour on square inches of nature.'[74]

His wife also exhibited there that year, a work entitled *Departing to Join Garibaldi*. The painting depicted the volunteers embarking on one of the Northern Italian lakes. The reviewer described the picture as 'very true and unaffectedly painted, but hung too high for proper examination'. This was not an uncommon occurrence, where the fate of many artists had been at the mercy of such decisions. 'Mr. Bridell's landscape in the hills above Como, between Varenna and Bellano, a picture of great merit, as far as we can judge at the height it is hung,' was a comment the following year.

The work entitled *Olive Gardens at Varenna* was exhibited at the Liverpool Academy and the Royal Academy in 1861. However the reviews of the painting were not as glowing as they had been in previous years. The subject was perhaps not so striking as those previously shown. Exhibited at the Liverpool Society for Fine Arts, the picture sold directly from there. This was to be the last of his large scale works. Thereafter, the artist seems to have adopted the preferred smaller format 50 x 35ins for his pictures. This growing taste for 'cabinet' pictures directly followed from the demands from patrons who were no longer seeking the grand impressive works beloved of the earlier Romantic painters.

There was also during July of this year, an event that the couple very likely attended. This was the sad duty of the funeral of Elizabeth Browning, in Florence. She had died on June 30th of that year, having contracted an infection, and due to her weak constitution, she was unable to shake it off. She is buried in the Protestant cemetery, in the monument there designed by Browning and Frederic Leighton.

Richard Ansdell was a well-known and successful member of the Royal Academy. In part his success was due to the popularity of the engravings of his work. He possessed a house in St. Albans Road Kensington, which had a sufficiently large garden for him to keep the animals that he used as models. He also owned a house in Lytham and a moor in Scotland. He had at this time, the leases of nos 7&8 Victoria Road, Kensington. Whether, through a private arrangement or through an agent, the Bridells negotiated to rent no 8 Victoria Road in 1862. However, it seems that although they were marked in the rate book for that year, in any event, they went abroad, and did not make payment. They returned for a short period in order to organise paintings for exhibition. Of their friends who were artists, we know they were on good terms with Frederick Smallfield and his family. Smallfield had attended the Royal Academy school and exhibited regularly there from 1849-1886. He was enthusiastically reviewed by Ruskin, which was probably due to the influence of the Pre-Raphaelites on his work. His two daughters, Beatrice and Rosalind, were also painters.

Another friend was William Burton, he was a member of the Society of Painters in Water-colour, exhibiting there in 1855 and earlier at the Royal Academy. As a very good friend of George Eliot, he travelled with her on the continent. In correspondence he praised Barbara Leigh Smith's exhibition of 1859; 'he didn't care about the want of finish in some of them – they had finer qualities than that of finish – he felt they were done on the spot under true inspiration.' He gave encouragement to Bridell, and attended the sale of his studio, purchasing

Bellagio Rock Lake Como
Courtesy of Fine Art Society, London.

several items. In 1874 he became Director of the National Gallery, a position which he held for 20 years.

1862 saw the opening in May of the International Exhibition in Kensington. It comprised of almost 800 British oil paintings and included *The Coliseum*. Alongside these massive exhibitions, an alternative way for the public to view works was also becoming popular. This was at a 'special viewing'. It provided income for an artist, which decreased his dependence on finding a buyer. Just as importantly, it offered subscribers the opportunity to list themselves as buyers of the future print, thus guaranteeing a viable return for the copyright holder. Holman Hunt was an artist who chose to show all of his works after 1860 in this manner. These viewings were held in London, over a matter of several weeks and generally advertised in the press. The public paid admission and if the work was popular the owner could expect to make a very lucrative return.

Narrative pictures, with themes depicting everyday life, were all the rage. Frith's *Day at the Seaside*, appearing at the Royal Academy in 1854, was soon followed by larger, more impressive achievements. *Derby Day* and *Paddington Station*, the latter being privately exhibited over a period of seven weeks and drew over 21,000 paid admissions. Tastes and styles in art were changing rapidly.

Bridell was moving away from the loftier themes of earlier subjects and portraying the everyday scene. These showed the working people, shepherds, fishermen, washerwomen, as part of their setting, but he nevertheless remained loyal to his inspiration, to portray Nature in her everchanging moods. His subjects were still on a grand scale. He was out of the mainstream and singleminded in his purpose. He would not adapt to the demands of 'modern art'. It is also to be remembered that very little of his work was seen publicly. He was away from London and had spent approximately only about eighteen months in the capital. He was not established as an artist there. It is not to be forgotten that there was inevitably, the consideration of competition. The London Post Office Directory lists 636 artists in 1855 and in 1860, 488 artists. The situation of artists, was, as always precarious. Only the fortunate few made a name for themselves, and this, by tradition, necessitated admission to the Royal Academy.

During this period, the artist completed other major works. Among these were, as a pair, *The Temple of Saturn* and *The Arch of Titus'* (50 x 35 ins.). ((These are untraced at the present time.) However, Bridell was no longer fortunate in having a patron and these pictures were acquired by picture dealer Joseph Morby.

He was also working on studies for a larger work, *Bellagio Rock (illus)* (30 x 54 ins., present location unknown). It appears that he completed two large versions on this theme. This work

Portrait
Reproduced courtesy of Mr. A.Cooper

illustrates most strikingly the confidence and mastery of Bridell. His love of skies is in evidence with clouds of trailing vapour, providing the spatial lightness and floating quality in which he excelled. Under the early evening light, the subtle tones of rock and water provide a delicate balance to the reflection of sky in the lake's darkening waters. The Rock dominates the lake with a timeless stillness. But in keeping with earlier themes, there is movement within the work which produces a satisfying harmony of contrasts. The fishing boats, manoeuvred by the straining oarsmen, move silently across the lake, against an impressive sky. The painting further demonstrates a richness and vibrancy in the use of colour. It is an image, which strikes us by its power and sheer brilliance of execution. It draws us into a sense of completeness of the harmony in the natural world.

He was now thirty two years of age, technically experienced and at the point at which his innate talent was finding its fullest expression. He may have been aware of how the demands of art had fatigued his body, but it seems he was even more driven in his determination to paint without ceasing. We can see the evidence of illness on his features from a photograph taken of Bridell during this time.

His long hours of toil resulted in debilitating phases of physical weakness. Tuberculosis was a highly contagious bacterial infection, generally found in poor and unhealthy conditions. In a healthy immune system the infection can lie dormant for years, but with tireless work and irregular eating habits, the disease takes hold, bringing tiredness, fever, and a persistant cough.

One of the few hospitals for the disease was at Brompton, treating 6000 outpatients in the year of 1861. The parents of Richard Parkes Bonington (1802-1828) had endeavoured to find treatment for their son but it was a futile search. Tuberculosis claimed the lives of between one in seven of the population during the mid-nineteenth century. Sadly, like Bridell, some of England's most gifted artists succumbed to the disease at an early age. Garnett, in the Life of W. J. Fox states that the consumption of which he died, was already firmly established before his marriage.[75] The only known treatment was a change of air, usually in the mountains. This provided the sufferer with respite from the debilitating effects of the illness. The disease brought periods of clarity and energy, alternated with periods of exhaustion. Bridell returned to his favourite locations on several occasions, in order to escape the heat of Rome, and where he was able breathe the cool mountain air. These were the Lakes of Northern Italy, and in particular, Lake Como.

As the heat of the summer grew more intense, the couple returned to England. Bridell continued to paint in the locality of Kensington, as evidenced by The Round Pond, Kensington Gardens. He also copied works by Turner in the Kensington Museum. We learn from Theodore Martin that he was intending to return to Rome to design a series of landscapes around the central theme of Rome's history. However, ironically and perhaps, with some premonition of the inevitable end of his life, Bridell completed *The Churchyard*. It is a striking, imaginative work of a graveyard overlooking the sea and has a very English 'feel'. It is reminiscent of a bay in the West Country and he may have visited the area in the hope of recuperation. The harmonious scene seems almost to suggest an acceptance of the nature of life itself. The silent flight of a group of birds out over the sea shore, is again a motif seen in other works by the artist.

The Brownings knew Eliza Fox's concern for her husband's health. Elizabeth records this in an undated letter to William Fox at an earlier time but it indicates that his health was in obvious decline before 1861, the year of her death.

> 'Dear Mr Fox, forgive all these wanderings. Give my love to your daughter, whose long continued anxiety about her husband I grieve to understand. May better

Churchyard by the Sea
Courtesy of Fine Art Society, London

accounts reach us soon. I don't think Rome agreed with him physically as well as it did aesthetically, and the English bracing air will give a better chance to his convalescence than he could get out of Italy....'

Robert Browning adds a note to this letter from his wife, 'Kind regards to Tottie and best wishes to her husband.'[76]

On August 20th 1863 in Kensington he died from consumption. As his wife recorded...'the long list of brilliant pictures which left his easel from that time (1858) until within 6 months of his death in 1863, give evidence of no failing power, and would have done credit to the industry of a far stronger man'.[77] What may have been achieved had he lived longer can never be known. His genius was recognised by some and it was recorded at the time that he was on the brink of receiving the recognition that he deserved.

His works provide the basis on which he should be reappraised. His achievement is not relative to a place in the history of art, but should be looked at in the light of his simple beginnings and total dedication to his love for beauty in landscape. In his pictures there is skill and sensitivity, which the subject and its expression eludes adequate description. The closest description of this quality is genius. It is an indefinable quality, recognisable only when it is found. In his best work there is an overriding perception of the harmony of all things finding its complete expression.

The following obituary appeared in *The Southampton Times* four days later.

> DEATH OF MR. F. L. BRIDELL
> It is with the deepest regret we announce to-day the death of our late talented townsman
>
> Mr F.L.Bridell, who was known to many of our readers as a painter of great merit, and who gave early promise of taking a leading place among the artists of the age, had his life been spared. Mr. Bridell has, we fear, like so many others before him, fallen a martyr to his love of art. From the earliest period of his life, the natural bent of his mind led him to study painting, and he followed up his inclination with all the zeal and disinterestedness of an enthusiast. He spent several years in Bavaria, studying from nature, and he also visited Rome, and other Italian cities to gather inspiration from the works of the great masters. His hand picture of 'The Colosseum by Moonlight' now in the collection of Mr J.H. Wolff of Bevois Mount was painted after a visit to Rome a few years back and was much admired at the exhibition of the Royal Academy. Mr.Wolff has also some other paintings by our deceased friend, and the Mayor has one which has been highly spoken of

by all who have seen it. Mr. Bridell's colouring is exquisite, and his works carry upon them the strong impression of unquestionable genius. He died at the early age of 32, leaving a widow of kindred tastes to lament his loss – a lady allied both by birth and marriage to the highest order of talent, the daughter of the splendid orator and honest politician, Mr. J. Fox, late MP for Oldham.

The loss to British art by his early death was recognised by Sir Theodore Martin. He had, we are told, given much encouragement and shown his appreciation of the artist's talent. Likewise, another leading Victorian artist, Sir Frederick Burton ranked amongst those who recognised the place the artist deserved. It is the following tribute by Sir Theodore Martin, which appeared in the *Art Journal* of 1864 that most poignantly sums up the artist's achievement attained during his short life span. He most eloquently expresses regret over the recognition which was deserved but never realised.

THE ART JOURNAL: JAN 1864

The premature close of the life of a man of genius is always sad but it is so in a preeminent degree when it comes before he had had the time or the opportunity to make his genius felt or to secure the recognition which alone compensates the artist for years of lonely struggle and nervous exhaustion. Raphael, Shelley, Keats and others it is true died young, yet, had they lived to a good age could they have made their "heritage of fame" one jot more secure? In their case there is little to regret. But the annals of art could they be written would tell of many a hand palsied in the prime of its power, just when the mastery over the materials of the art had been gained and when the strong poetic soul had begun to show with free and fluent pencil how nature was mirrored within it and how well and wisely it read and could interpret the deep significance of:

> "The power, the beauty, and the majesty
> That have their haunts by dale, or piney mountain,
> Or forest, by slow stream or pebbly spring.
> Or chasms and watery depths."

Not a few such pass away leaving a name utterly unknown except it may be by some stray connoisseur. Others like Bonington and Muller among painters, or Schubert among musicians, rise rapidly into renown; but only when recognition comes too late to quicken the pulses or lighten the heart of the men who have done so much for the enjoyment of others. Of this number, we fear was Mr. Bridell, for although within a certain circle his works were known and appreciated, the time had not come when his fine powers which latterly were ripening with striking rapidity, must have forced a general recognition and placed him in the very foremost rank of poetical landscape painters.

He early showed a talent for painting and began life in his native town as a portrait painter. His early efforts were wholly unassisted; Southampton at the time had not the resources of supplying even the elements of an education in art. While Mr.Bridell was in his 16th year, his works attracted the attention of a picture cleaner and dealer who was visiting Southampton at the time.

He induced him to enter into one of those engagements by which young men of real power have not infrequently bartered for a bare subsistence brains, time, and health. Whether Mr.Bridell's engagement was of this one sided nature, we do not pretend to say. It secured for him at all events, the means of a prolonged study abroad, the fruits of which were conspicuous in the artist's best works. But on the other hand, a mistaken view of self-interest on the part of his employer, kept him back from the London public, long after he ought to have been winning a place among the artists of the British School.

It was not until 1858 that Mr.Bridell exhibited in London when he produced a marked impression by his fine picture of *The Coliseum by Moonlight*, exhibited in that year at the R.A. and again last year at the International Exhibition. There was in this picture the unmistakeable presence of an eye that looked at nature with the sympathies of a poet and a hand that dealt with what it undertook in a fashion of its own and that no common one. The impression then made Mr. Bridell fully sustained by his subsequent works. A visit the following year to the North Italian lakes resulted in several noble pictures. There were eagerly sought after by the lovers of Art whom circumstances threw across his path. Mr. John Platt and Mr. Josiah Radcliffe possess two specimens of a very large size, while Sir Theodore Martin and others, may be mentioned as the owners of many smaller pictures from the same field, all distinguished by consummate truth, combined with poetical and perfectly original treatment. There was nothing small or trivial in Mr. Bridell's representations of nature. He did not fritter away your attention upon the foliage of a fern or the details of a fence. He placed the grand panorama of plain forest, lake, mountain and sky vividly before you, made you look at it with his eyes, contemplate it with his mood and feel their influences on the whole scene as he himself had felt them. He was not put out by nature. On the contrary he never feared to grapple with her in her coyest or grandest moods.

It is impossible to look at his pictures and not to feel that at his easel, and while his imagination was most active, nature was ever before his eyes and that he was bent to fix her varied features upon his canvas with that individuality of stamp which is their subtlest charm, but for which so many are content to substitute merely conventional types. In his painting of skies and clouds in particular, Mr. Bridell seems to us to occupy a place amongst British artists only second to Turner: some of his earlier works may be open to the charge of heaviness in treatment, but this cannot be alleged against any of this later pictures. We have present to our minds as we write, several, which bear the same place in our memory as the actual sunrises and sunsets, twilights and moonlights of which every lover of nature carries a store in his memory as revelations of nature never to be forgotten.

In the shifting aspect of the clouds, in the gorgeous lives of the dawn and twilight, in the trailing vapours of lakes and mountains, Mr. Bridell obviously revelled. He possessed the art of preserving in his colours all the transparency and airy lightness of reality. His best pictures impress us with the same sense of beauty and completeness as fine poems or a fine strain of music, and we speak from experience when we say that a picture in his best manner will make you forget that you are looking at it in a London room and lose yourself in the solemn sweetness of after sunset upon the Lake of Como or a summer dream of the olive clad slopes of the wind swept Soracte.

Unfortunately for his fame, most of Mr. Bridell's best works have never been exhibited. Chief among these is a landscape of an important size (painted in emulation of Turner, as Turner had painted in emulation of Claude) illustrative of Spenser's description in 'The Faerie Queene' of the Temple of Love. It was commissioned by Mr. Wolff of Bevois Mount House, Southampton and justifies the artist's ambitious hope of rivalling, without imitating, his great predecessor. Mr. Wolff was among the first to appreciate the rising genius of Mr. Bridell. He bought largely of him and this collection, containing among others, The Coliseum, is fine and important enough to merit the title of 'The Bridell Gallery' which Mr. Wolff has given it. This gentleman we believe, courteously allows lovers of art to inspect his collection. Another large picture entitled "Sunset on the Atlantic" exhibited six years ago in Liverpool produced an impression there, which has never been forgotten. This picture also has not been seen in London. In 1858 Mr. Bridell married in Rome the daughter of Mr. W. J. Fox, then MP for Oldham. The lady herself an artist and this union was one of those rare marriages of sympathy almost ideal. For sometime past it has been painfully apparent to Mr. Bridell's friends that his health was seriously shaken. He continued however to work on hopefully and contemplated making another visit to Rome this Autumn to carry out a design for a series of landscapes illustrative of the rise, grandeur and decay of Rome which he had long had in contemplation. To this series his Coliseum shrouded in gloom and shadow, with malarial mists veiling its base, would have formed as he intended, the appropriate close.

Mr. Bridell died of consumption at the early age of 32. His fame naturally sensitive and delicate, had we fear been overtasked. In his passionate enjoyment of his art he seemed to forget that the body has its claim as well as the spirit and ever after the dilated pupil and hollow cheek gave token to his friends of the insidious bane that was sapping his life.

We have known him go on working at his easel without intermission for periods that would have taxed the energies of the strongest man. Two of his latest pictures were parted for the last R.A. exhibition but were returned. This as all the world now knows was no disgrace. Disappointment it certainly was. He bore it bravely but we shall not soon forget the pang we felt when as he showed us with a half timid satisfaction these beautiful pictures and told us of the rejection. We looked at the worn face and the eager eyes to which disease had already begun to give a painful brightness and thought that this perhaps last chance of reading his success in the admiring eyes of his fellowmen had been denied him by the miserable selfishness of those who thrust out true art from the walls of the Academy to make room for vulgar commonplace and repetitions of effects, that have been stale for years. It is easy to understand how little pictures so full of bold originality could be appreciated by those who have long since lost sight of nature in the tricks of a vicious mannerism. In that great school of poetic landscape Art, in which Turner, Constable, Muller are the leaders and has its representatives among Frenchmen in Daubigne, Rousseau, Francais, Ziem, Flandrin and others, Mr. Bridell has already taken foremost rank. Had he lived he must have earned a European reputation; and numerous and fine as are the works he has left, his early death is in the interests of art, deeply to be deplored. We have only to add that in manners, Mr. Bridell was simple, amiable and modest. Firm without self-assertion, sincere without being obtrusive, we can believe he was beloved by his friends as most certainly he was respected by those whose knowledge of him was comparatively slight.

Sir Theodore Martin

~ EPILOGUE ~

Bridell's simple will, which had been drawn up in 1859, left his wife as the sole beneficiary. He had become by his death, not a wealthy man but certainly enjoying a comfortable life-style. His personal effects, comprising of a great number of ornamental items and furniture,were gathered, in the main from the continent. These items and the contents of his studio, were in the Christie's auction of 26th February 1864, which was held for the benefit of his widow. The contents of the artist's studio included some 70 studies in oil, approximately 45 of these in gilt frames and realising reasonable sums. Amongst the items sold were 14 sketches, English and Italian scenes by Bonington. In itself this fact is something of a puzzle, which may never be solved. Bonington died two years before Bridell was born. There is a slight possibility that he may have purchased them from a dealer, but this seems unlikely. He may have been given them in exchange for some of his own work. It is possible that he was given them by James Duffield Harding, who had produced engravings of Bonington's work but this does seem unlikely.

An auction at Christies's the following year, 23/5/1865 contained twelve pictures by Bridell. Approximately five of these appear to be early works, and were executed in the region of the Thames. Of the larger works sold, there was the pair *A Forest of Stone Pines on Fire* and *Charcoal Burning at the Wilde-Kaiser Mountain,* (50 x34 ins) both dated 1856. Also included was the *Outskirts of Varenna* (50 x30 ins) 1861 which had been exhibited at the British Institution in 1862. These pictures were possibly from the provenance of Mr. Wiseman of Southampton, who made the frames for some of the artist's pictures.

Bridell, after his death, still commanded some interest in London. An advertisement appeared in *The Times* and for several weeks in March and April following the sale, Bridell's major achievement, was on view to the public. '*The Temple of Venus*', described as 'a masterpiece of art' could be seen by the public at the Gallery of Messrs Moore McQueen & Co. 25 Berners Street London. It then passed into the Douglas collection. Subsequently it was mentioned in the Review of the collection of Andrew Kurtz, Wavertree, Liverpool in the Athenaeum 12/09/1885. This gentleman 'allowed most liberal access to his private collection' which contained some of the most impressive works by living artists. It was described in the article, as Bridell's best work. In the sale of the Kurtz collection by Christies in May 1891, the Temple of Venus was sold to King, Liverpool. The present whereabouts of this grand work have not been traced.

James Wolff and his wife, three children, three servants and a nurse resided in Southampton until the death of his wife in 1867. A few years later, he remarried and moved to Upper Norwood, near London. James Wolff succumbed to consumption in 1876. Unfortunate circumstances it seems necessitated the sale of the contents of the Bridell Gallery on 27th February 1864 at Christies. This was the whole collection of paintings by Bridell that Wolff had acquired. It is to be regretted that these works would never been seen in entirety again. Bridell's simple gravestone in Brompton cemetery has been eroded and weathered. There is no visible memorial to this forgotten artist.

★ ★ ★

The death of her husband, and the following year, that of her father, was a double blow to Eliza Fox. She made a lengthy visit to Algiers, staying with Eugene and Barbara Bodichon. Here she made some impression of her talent and was commissioned to paint several portraits of notables of the country. By 1869 she had returned to Kensington, and was living in Campden Hill Road. She remarried, in 1871, George Edward Fox, her cousin, with whom she had travelled to Rome in 1858. She was, once again, Eliza Fox but continued to exhibit under the name of Bridell-Fox. She presented the bust of Bridell, which had been commissioned from Richard Cockle Lucas in Romsey, to the Hartley Institute. The Institute was opened in 1862 and was the foundation for Southampton University. The bust is now in the ownership of the Southampton Museum archives.

Very little of Mrs Eliza Bridell-Fox is recorded, apart from her exhibiting annually, from this time until her death. She wrote a few articles, based around her art, which was published in the *Girls Own Paper* and a recollection of the young Robert Browning published in *Argosy* in 1890. She was nevertheless aware of a revival of interest in her late husband which occurred in Southampton in early 1888.

In January 1888 she wrote to *The Southampton Times*, following the first of Rose's letters, and shed more light on the circumstances surrounding her meeting with her first husband and her husband's health.

Sir,

I see with great pleasure that the name of Mr. Frederick Lee Bridell is not forgotten in the place of his birth. It is very gratifying to know that his fellow townsmen appreciated his character and genius – a genius that was capable of raising itself from the lowest state of society to the highest.

I write to say that should your excellent idea be carried out, of a local exhibition of

Signatures of Bridell, and his wife

Mr. Bridell's works, I beg that the committee will put themselves into communication with me, as I believe that I could indicate to them in what quarters to apply for the loan of some of his best works. I myself still possess a few choice watercolours (20 of which have just returned from the Jubilee exhibition at Manchester) which I should be happy to lend, as well as a few small but brilliant studies in oil.

I should like to correct the impression made by his friend Mr. Rose as to Mr. Bridell's health. It gave way, as Mr. Rose says, with the anxiety he suffered at the time of his differences with Mr. Holder, the dealer to whom he had bound himself; but when I first made his acquaintance in London in 1858, just before he started for Rome, his health had revived. The long list of large brilliant pictures which left his easel from that time until within 6 months of his death, in 1863, give evidence of no failing power, and would have done credit to the industry of a far stronger man.

As a matter of detail I should also like to correct the statement that the small sketches and studies for pictures sold by me shortly after his death realised the sum Mr. Rose named. Individually they fetched good prices; but the fact is that the whole total of the sale did not amount to nearly half the sum mentioned, and half of that again was from other sources.

Yours truly
Eliza F.Bridell-Fox
4 Campden Hill Rd, Kensington.   18/1/1888

Although the writer states here that twenty pictures were returned, in fact only four pictures were displayed at the Exhibition. These were:

Lake Como	loaned by	S R Platt
Returning from the Wedding Upper Austria		E Naylor Esq
On Lake Como		Mrs E F Fox
Varenna		Mrs EF Fox

Eliza Bridell-Fox continued to exhibit at the Society for Female Artists, which was inaugurated in 1857. Ernest Gambart had opened a gallery in 1854. Eliza Bridell-Fox and Madame Bodichon had four of their own exhibitions here until 1866. Eliza Fox died in Kensington in 1903. There are references to pictures and sketches in her will, with a request that these be sold and the proceeds used to pay out her requests and expenses. Her younger brother, Franklin, had died in Wellington, Somerset the previous year. He had been residing with the family of Alfred Damp. In her will, Eliza left a small sum to Hester Damp, who was recorded in the 1901 census as living in Paddington and working as a civil servant. The Damp family seem to have been regarded by Eliza as 'extended family' though there is no evidence of blood ties between them.

Edwin Holder also died suddenly in February 1864, near Wakefield in Yorkshire. He had returned with his family in 1860 to York, and had advised on the acquisition and restoration of paintings for numerous country houses in the area. After his death, his daughter Charlotte submitted lists of paintings by Bridell to various prospective purchasers. Whether some of these completed works did not bear signatures or had signatures attached to the rear of the picture, it is impossible to say. Nor can we be certain that a signature was not completed by another hand following Bridell's death. Charlotte and her mother later moved to Hereford. Both succumbed to bronchitis in February of 1890. Charlotte at this time was 59 years of age and unmarried. In her will she left her not inconsiderable legacy (about £1500) to the children of her cousin, the artist Edward Henry Holder.

In 1904, the Hartley Institute held an exhibition entitled *The Relics of Old Southampton*. Henry Rose (now eighty) loaned a portrait of Bridell dated 1855, that he owned, as well as a painting entitled *On the Rhine*, a sketch by Bridell, and his own portrait of 1848– which had been so important in Bridell's career. A collector of Art and a leading figure in the town was Mr. William Burrough Hill. He loaned to the exhibition another portrait of Bridell and of this picture, we have no further detail.

Mr Burrough Hill, was instrumental in returning the lost *Coliseum by Moonlight* to Southampton in 1929. He had a Bridell collection at his home in Regents Park Road and bequeathed much of the collection to the people of Southampton after his death. He also completed a short booklet entitled *An Appreciation of the Coliseum by Moonlight*, the major part of which is included here, as testimony to his conviction and belief in Bridell's talent.

SOUTHERN DAILY ECHO 13/4/1949
Bridell's Lost Masterpiece was sold with household fittings

The discovery was a chance in a million probably. For many years that veteran art lover, Mr.William Burrough Hill, had sought a picture by one who is probably Southampton's greatest artist F.L.Bridell. The picture was painted in Rome in 1859 and is considered to be the masterpiece of Bridell who beginning as a house painter in Southampton at 15s a week, rose by sheer force of genius to high rank among English artists, dying at the early age of 33.

This great picture The Coliseum at Rome by Moonlight had passed through various hands and had last been noted at an exhibition in Nottingham in 1913. Since then it had vanished from public view. In his search, Mr.W.B.Hill had followed every clue in vain. Then, as is the way of things it was most unexpectedly discovered.

By the merest coincidence I happened to be spending a weekend with friends in a residential hotel on Denmark Hill, London. As we entered the winter garden my attention was immediately caught by a magnificent picture, the subject of which seemed familiar somehow.

"Surely, that is a Lee Bridell?" I asked my friends. They did not know, so we went up, looked for a signature and there it was!

I had often seen the small copy of the picture at Mr.B.Hill's house in his collection there; could this actually be the long sought original?

Immediately on my return home I told him of my "find".

His eyes always bright flashed with excitement. Down went the name and address of the hotel, written in pencil on his white shirt cuff, as was his custom.

Very early next morning, he set off to London by car with all the enthusiasm of youth. (He was by then 84 years old – for this was in 1929).

Arriving at the hotel he had a chat with the proprietor, viewed the picture and bought it then and there. A treasure which crowned his collection of Bridell's works. He said afterwards that this was one of the greatest moments of his life.

The way in which the picture reached the hotel is rather amusing. The proprietor had purchased a house in Dulwich and one of the conditions of sale was that this huge picture be taken over with the house as part of the fittings, the vendor not knowing what to do with it.

The transaction completed, the hotel proprietor very wisely moved the picture to more suitable surroundings in the lovely old Georgian house which had become his hotel and there, by the strangest of chances I happened to see it.

Through Mr. Burrough Hill this Southampton masterpiece returned to the hometown of its creator. And now, after its many wanderings, it hangs where it belongs, in a place of honour in the Art Gallery of Southampton.

Elsie M.Sandell

It is to Mr. William Burrough Hill that we owe a debt of gratitude. Due to his generosity some of Bridell's work is in the public domain, including the magnificent Coliseum.

THE COLISEUM AT ROME BY MOONLIGHT by William Burrough Hill

The genius of his day, Bridell was one of Southampton's greatest artists. The word "born artist" describe him truthfully and essentially, for he was one of the most spontaneous artists that ever lived. Lay figures and other conventional models had no attraction for him. He was concerned with realities; thirsting for natural beauty, it was to nature that he went direct for his subjects – storm-driven clouds, a moon-lit ruin, or the midnight sun. He did not portray battles or scenes of revelry; for him the plunging sea or the mountain summit – and possibly no painter has ever realised more fully the words "and the firmament showeth His handywork". He was pre-occupied with the wonders and perfections neither wrought nor touched by the hand of man. A lurid sunset, an approaching storm thrilled him with delight, and this strong emotion he conveyed to his canvas, so that those who look at his pictures feel the grandeur of the scene in some measure as he felt it. Sometimes they almost persuade themselves that they can hear the roar of the thunder or taste the salt spray.

"The Coliseum at Rome by Moonlight" was painted when the frail young artist was at the very zenith of his power; it was the culmination of his talent and almost his final work.

That "noble wreck in ruinous perfection", the Coliseum, crumbling, colossal, weird in the moonlight, gave full play to his fancy and to his power of portraying light, shade, darkness and fitful illumination. It is fascinating to us to contemplate the appeal that such a subject must have made to this essentially romantic man, with his highly-strung temperament and delicate frame. A partially starlit sky, the moon combatting as it were, the attempted obscuration by wind-driven cloud banks- scattered and whirled in almost volcanic disruption, the moonbeams piercing the crevices of the nimbus and the shafts of light striking through the windowless apertures of the gaunt, dismantled, lichen grown pile, once the scene

74

of luxurious revelry, now still with the savour of death in its silence- a silence broken only by the screech of some tempest-driven bird. Long since passed away that wild gaiety and abandonment to pleasures unlovely and cruel, but the lovely building has not yet faded into nothingness (for even human wrought beauty tends to endure) and above are the Heavens declaring the glory of God. Bridell was a poet in the wide sense of the word. His mind was steeped in poetry- that indefinable quality which has been most nearly described as "the finer spirit and breath of all knowledge."

His early death was one of the greatest losses ever sustained by the art world. Brimful of natural art of the very highest standard, he died at the age of 33. By his works he is known. But where are they? Very little is left to remind the people of the ancient grey-walled town of Southampton of his birth, his work, or his death. That miserable little tenement in which he first saw the light has fallen and there is no monument or tablet to his memory, scarcely a relative or friend alive to remember him. " If you wish to see my monument, look around " runs the famous epitaph to Sir Christopher Wren, so it must be with Bridell; but where are we to look? There are a few of his works in our Art Gallery; and some of these are well worthy of his name. But few men are prophets in their own country. I believe that in Yorkshire a collector once had a Bridell gallery. Dying so young, the artist's fame had little time to spread. Compare him to our great artist, William Shayer, who lived to be 92! Yet during his short span Bridell in Rome and elsewhere, working and studying, plodding so assiduously that he seldom paused for rest or praise. Many people think that he was conscious of the delicacy of the frame which held the priceless jewel of genius and felt it well to pursue his avocation almost madly while the light lasted. When he was no more the great Art world awoke, and amazed at his works, said: Who was this man? He had no title, no string of letters to his name. But without such honours his works, like water, found their level. The connoisseurs clamoured for his canvasses and biddings ran fast and high at Christie's for the short life's work of this simple and almost unknown Southampton lad. I have a strong conviction that if "names" could be eliminated, the works of Frederick Lee Bridell, judged impartially for real merit, would stand out as the highest of our comparative modern painters, not even excepting Turner. A bold opinion to venture of the poor lad who was a page-boy and afterwards a house-painter at 15/- a week! But his talents were of the rarest type, such as no conscious training or steady perseverance could ever vie with. How shall a man learn to represent nature in such a way that the panorama of plain, forest, lake, mountain and sky is brought before us, so truly and vividly that we look at it with his eyes, contemplate it in his mood, feel its influences as he felt them? Had he been spared to a ripe old age, he could not have made his heritage to fame one jot more secure. Born to work unseen and to die so young! But graduations of light, flashes, streaks of colour, radiance of the sun, sheen of the moon, glitter of stars, these were his to transfer to canvas by a miraculous method. He was wont to rush out with ecstasy to paint a stormy sky and a silhouetted landscape tinged with crimson and gold-scenes as brilliant and as transient as his life. So true a master he was of pigments and mediums that most of his works are almost as fresh today as they were when he painted them some sixty years since. Bridell prophesied of his painting of Spenser's Faerie Queene that it should hang between the two pictures (which it resembled in size) of Claude Lorraine and Turner — a prophecy unfulfilled as yet. His picture of the "Woods of Sweet Chestnut above Varenna, Lake Como" was presented to the National Gallery by his widow; it is now at the Tate Gallery.

(Here Burrough-Hill includes comments from the Art Journal obituary and the whole of the letter written by Bridell from Rome in December 1858), he continues:

Grand indeed was the actual building of the Coliseum of Rome — though it was the hotbed of vice and cruelty, and its vicious career was pursued for some few centuries until the monk Telemachus leaped into the Arena and beseeched in the name of god to stop the wickedness while the Christian Church prevailed through his protestations, and his body was torn to pieces, but this sacrifice was crowned in glory, as was proved by this being the last gladiatorial show in Rome.

All this Bridell read and studied during the time in which he was at work on his most wonderful picture. Small matter for surprise then that the painting should stir us, even so deeply as it does. We cannot forget it; it haunts the mind as surely as it enchants the eye. We are compelled to think about it. We are stirred by the emotion that moved the artist. In accordance with our capacity for swift and delicate response, we receive his mood and know his thoughts. His sensitive mind and his sympathy were the medium. We hear the phrase " the unselfishness of great art" and we realise that these are not empty words, when we see how Bridell gave not only his extraordinary talent and skill, but himself to the making of his pictures.

~ ENDNOTES ~

1   May-July 1975

2   10 June-12 July 1968

3   Obituary reprinted in full at end

4   Reynolds p 155

5   Life of W.J,Fox. P311

6   20/06/2005 lot 44

7   Rose.loc.cit

8   Ibid.

9   Ibid.

10   This information from a descendant of Bridell's sister, Mr Douglas

11   Rose. loc.cit

12   Letter 7/5/1815 The Examiner

13   Beaumont.May1808.Wordsworth Library,Grasmere.

14   Lamp of Beauty p8

15   PPA. p1

16   Art Journal 1850 p181

17   Art Journal May 1851

18   The Royal Academy Review

19   Memoir by Skilton p1. OWCS Annual 1963

20   Article .The Portfolio 1880

21   See George Landow.www.victorianweb.org.Nature's Infinite Variety. reprinted from the Journal of Aesthetics and Art Criticism 38 (1970)

22   JCLE Vol. 1 p.273

23   Gambart p89

24   Pre-Raphelite Diaries & Letters. P205 cited by Robertson p354

25   Victorian Art World in Photographs. p93

26   Christies sale 27/2/1864

27   PPA.preface

28   Letter to Sir Charles Winn. West Yorkshire Archives Service WYL1352/A1/8/18 reproduced courtesy of Lord St.Oswald.

29   ibid.

30   Rose.loc.cit

31   Ibid.

32   Ibid.

33   Handlist of Painters. P2.

34   Diary p78

35   Maas. p48

36   AJ 1850 p181

37   Athenaeum 1857 p410

38   Letter in National Art Library, V&A .

39   JCLE Vol.2 p 83

40   Southampton Times 21.1.1888

41   Confirmed by Swiss Railways.

42   CLE Robertson. p12

43   F& IN p281

44   JCLE Vol.2. p96

45   EBB Huxley p315

46   EBB. Huxley p303

47   F&IN. P206/7

48   JCLE Vol2 p106

49   F&IN.p183

50   NEI Hawthorne p198

51   NEI. p361

52   LEBBA p313

53   LEBBA .Letter 202

54   LMG.letter 79

55   Bessie Rayner Parkes.Girton College Papers 6/56.Cambridge

56   LMG letter 404

57   LMG .letters no 419 (W.Fox),421 and 422

58   Ibid. no 428

59   EBBL. Huxley. p225

60   Argosy Feb. 1890

61   Lawrences. Crewkerne.16/5/03 l.975

62   Letters to J.Ruskin John Rylands 1972. Whether the meeting occurred has not been verified. Ruskin left for the continent on May 20 spending 5 months abroad.

63   Art Journal 1860 p78

64   LMG letter 455

65   Ibid. letter 428

66   GSJ.Colloms

67   Art Journal 1860 May

68   Apollo.Aug 1974

69   Sold Christies 29/3/1984 mistitled, Grotto of Neptune.

70   Christies.13/5/1977

71   Panton p54

72   Panton p112

73   JCLE.p26.

74   Art Journal 1864 p347

75   Garnett p311

76   Life of WJFox.p322

77   Soton Times.21/1/1888

~ APPENDIX ~

Rosa Bonheur (1822–1899)

Rosa Bonheur had been suddenly projected into the limelight in France when her major work *The Horse Fair*, was exhibited at The Salon in 1853. Critics and the public flocked to see this epic piece which measured approx 8 x13 ft.

Ernest Garmbart, the Belgian print-seller and picture dealer, seizing the opportunity, was to introduce Rosa Bonheur and the picture to the British public in 1855. The response was 'a unanimous concert of admiration'. The painting 'went on tour' for three years which included the United States. *The Horse Fair* now rests in New York at the Metropolitan Museum of Art, a gift from Cornelius Vanderbilt in 1887.

William Powell Frith, had caught the public's attention with the exhibition of *Day at the Seaside* at the Royal Academy in 1854. His next work *Derby Day* was eagerly anticipated, and on view to the public in 1858.

James Duffield Harding (1797–1863)

Producing picturesque views for engravings provided a steady income for a number of watercolour artists, Harding, in particular besides William Callow and James Holland. These artists were more fortunate to escape the fate of their predecessors, who had struggled to make a living. They became well-established, owning houses in the London suburbs and enjoying a reasonable level of prosperity. By the 1850's the market was however moving in another direction and prints depicting popular works of the day were in demand.

Henry Holiday in his autobiography describes an incident some years later involving J. D. Harding:

> 'My father's friend Mons. A Roche, had established an original kind of educational institution in which the leading professors of various subjects gave lectures and lessons, and ladies could attend courses on one or more subjects as they pleased. A drawing class was held by J.D.Harding, who ranked the best drawing master of the time and as Ruskin had been one of his pupils and always treated his work with respect, we may take it that he had ability. His class was getting too full and he

suggested the formation of a junior class, which Mons Roche invited me to take, if I could come to an understanding with Mr.Harding. My parents had given me every facility but it was clear I ought not to miss an opportunity of earning something, and I called on my "prospective boss". He received me courteously but with a scrutinising glance and after a few general enquiries asked what I was then doing. I had just returned from Swanage and I said I had been painting a large landscape from nature. Had I been a diplomatist, I should have worded my statement differently. "What" he said "are you a Pre-Raphaelite?" "I am". The diplomatic sky darkened and his face was itself a declaration of war. He at once attacked what he assumed to be my main body, viz., Mr Ruskin, and opened fire with two charges. 1st, that the writing of his renegade pupil were a mass of pernicious heresies; and 2nd, that they were merely a re-cook of his (Mr Harding's) own work on art. Indeed he assured me that his friends asked him why he allowed Ruskin to publish his (Mr Harding's) books under a new title "Modern painters" and under his (Mr. Ruskin's) name. I though I detected a slight inconsistency between the two propositions, and that if the question were to be settled by argument I might leave them to demolish each other. But he was master of the situation, he had the big battalions, and though I could not surrender, the battle for me was lost. M. Roche wrote to me that Mr Harding had been so upset by what I suppose was his first encounter with a live Pre-Raphaelite, that for some unaccountable reason, he withdrew from the whole thing; upon which they offered, and I accepted, the senior class.'

Photography

The rapid development of the processes involved led to important advances in photography. In 1855, a photograph of the stand at Epsom was to aid Frith in his painting of *Derby Day*. Elizabeth Barrett Browning records a photograph taken of her husband in 1857 and the artist David Roberts records his photograph being taken in the winter of 1860. By the 1860's photographic exhibitions were regular events.

W.H.Bartlett (1809-1854)

From his drawings made in Switzerland approx 20,000 copies of *Travels in Switzerland* were sold. He supplied drawings of the British Isles, the Continent (travelled on four occasions to) the United States, Canada, Turkey Asia Minor, Syria, Italy Greece, Egypt, Sinai and the Arabian Desert. In all he produced 19 volumes of drawings. His endless travels, in order to support a wife and five children in England, were undertaken however with considerable regard for his health and comfort. We are told: 'He was always most particular in the food he took; he travelled comfortably, taking with him an iron bedstead and tent; chose good localities to sleep upon – places distant from swampy ground. He paid his servants so much per day, to find him in horses and everything requisite for the journey. He was very much satisfied with his guide, and delivered him at parting a certificate to that effect. He always carried with him his own tea, the only beverage he made use of in his travels.' He died at the age of 44 from an unknown illness on returning from Asia Minor and was buried at sea.

Robert Browning (1812-89)

Robert Browning also attempted play-writing. An historical tragedy *Strafford* was produced at the Theatre Royal Covent Garden in 1837. The venture was not a success and Browning was 'a good deal annoyed at the go of things behind the scenes and vowed to never write another play again.' although he did not keep to his intention. Interesting in this connection is the fact that the future wife of Theodore Martin, Helen Faucit, took the leading female part of the Countess of Carlisle.

Ernest Gambart (1814-1902)

Ernest Gambart, the Belgian print seller arrived in England in 1840. Jeremy Maas writes 'Within 30 years Ernest Gambart, more than any other individual, transformed the London art world.'

It was the upturn in the art market, occurring in the late 1840's which in turn led to increasing wealth for the artists, print-sellers and dealers. On the back of this rising tide, it was the print-sellers themselves who were becoming the 'nouveau-riche'. The steel plate had replaced copper and greater quantities of reproductions were now possible from one plate. The print-sellers were bringing the images of popular art and the new found reputations of living artists into nearly every home in the country.

The implications for the patron, if he was commissioning a work had now a new consideration. This in turn would influence the artist and the way he was to portray the subject. Would the subject make for an interesting and popular print? If the subject matter translated well into engraving, then the copyright itself could become a valuable asset. In turn this meant a new distinction for the art market. A painting could be sold to one individual. He could purchase the copyright himself, or the copyright could be sold to another, as a separate entity. For Landseer, the sale of copyrights for prints was a lucrative business, and he benefitted considerably from it. William Powell Frith was also an artist who gained financially from the popularity of his prints. The copyright for Frith's *Derby Day* was purchased by Gambart even before the picture was painted. It was an added consideration that in some cases the exhibition rights could also be sold as a separate entity, and considerable sums could be made from the entrance fees to view a single work.

William Johnson Fox (1786-1864)

William Johnson Fox was born in Suffolk, the son of a peasant-farmer. His father gave up his tenancy when the boy was a few years old, and took up several occupations, in an effort to earn a living. Both he and his wife were strict Calvinists. At thirteen years of age, William Fox commenced work as a bank clerk. In his leisure time, he studied Latin, Greek and mathematics. He took to writing for prizes in essays, and occasionally wrote for the local paper. In 1806, at twenty years he entered the Independent College at Homerton to become a Minister of the Church, and in 1810 took up his first post in Fareham. After much deliberation over the Unitarian controversy, he broke entirely with the orthodox Church. Two years later he became a Minister of the Unitarian chapel at Chichester. Here in Chichester, he became engaged to the daughter of a barrister, Eliza Florance. He had become, within the matter of a few years, a consummate rhetorician, and had published numerous sermons. The recognition of his preaching ability resulted in a chapel being built specially for him in South Place, Finsbury. At this time he was also making regular contributions to The Norwich Mercury. Gradually becoming more involved with literature and politics, he began to move away from his earlier theological preoccupations.

The leading publication of the Unitarian denomination was *The Monthly Repository* of which he had become the joint editor with Robert Apsland. It was a theological publication until William Fox purchased the copyright in 1831 and as his daughter later describes 'he endeavoured to raise it from its original denominational character into a first-class literary and political journal….as such it was a forerunner, distinctly in advance of its time'. His interests now were evolving into a more active role and he took a prominent part in agitating for political reform as a leading member of the Anti-Corn Law League. *The Monthly Repository* also included literary and philosphical articles, amongst the contributors were John Stuart Mill and Crabb Robinson. Fox also gave weekly lectures to the National Hall of Working Mens Association in Holborn. In these, he embraced a very wide range of topics, from moral, social, political and literary which testified to a man with a marvellous capacity to absorb and also to dispense knowledge. The main objective of his ambition was for a movement for secondary education.

In his personal life however, he was not so successful. Due to differences of temperament, Fox separated from wife when Eliza was 12years of age. She insisted that she remain with her father and brother Florence, and they subsequently moved to a house in Bayswater. William Fox resided here with his children and a ward, Eliza Flower. Eliza's second brother, Franklin resided with their mother until he became a seaman. It appears there was little contact between Eliza and her mother following the separation.

William Fox left the editorship of the *Repository*, but continued to make contributions to *The Times* and later *The Morning Chronicle*. His lectures to the working classes between 1844-6 were later collected into four volumes. These lectures, and the admiration gained from his Anti-Corn Law League speeches resulted in an invitation to stand for the constituency of Oldham. After a closely run contest, he was returned as Member of Parliament in 1847. He held this seat, barring two short breaks until his retirement in 1863. Having himself triumphed over the disadvantages of humble beginnings, he gave all his energy to benefit the working classes.

Eliza Florance Fox (1824–1903)

Eliza Fox, in the mould of her father, was a pioneer. She had received a good general education upto the age of sixteen. However, she was determined to pursue a career as an artist, and avidly painted portraits of those who would sit for her. Women at this time, were not allowed to attend University or seek admission to the Royal Academy school. It was generally thought that too much education was not good for women. She persisted in her determination until a friend of her fathers persuaded him that she should attend instruction. At Sass's School in Charlotte Street, Bloomsbury, Eliza met Anna Mary Howitt (daughter of the writer and translator Mary Howitt), Holman Hunt and Rossetti. Conducted by a Mr. Cary it was one of the few schools open to women. Anna Howitt went to Munich for further study and took drawing lessons from Professor von Kaalbach. Her siser Margaret later wrote a biography of Overbeck, the founder of the Nazarene group.

On completion of her course, Eliza gave drawing classes in the library of her father's house in Bedford Square. The class in itself was ground-breaking. Nudity was a topic that inflamed opinions and discussion in all branches of the creative arts. For the first time female students in London were able to study the undraped figure. She established herself as an artist with subject pictures and portraits working from a small studio in her home. In 1859, Eliza Fox and her fellow artists campaigned for the admission of women to the Royal Academy schools with the result that one of her students, Laura Herford, was finally accepted in 1860. Her acceptance paved the way for educational privileges without prejudice for all talented individuals.

Barbara Leigh Smith Bodichon (1827–1891)

Barbara Leigh Smith did not receive any formal art training. Her status as a professional artist was established therefore when Ernest Gambart offered her a solo exhibition in French Gallery in 1859. She was the daughter of a Unitarian minister. Her biographer, Hirsch describes her as 'born into a wealthy and cultured family on whom fortune smiled'.

Barbara Leigh Smith and Elizabeth Whitehead founded the Portman Hall School in London. They had private incomes and personal freedom and used their talents and influence to obtain opportunities for those less able to rectify the deficiencies in the legal system, and to a lesser degree, that of education. This innovative school accepted children of all social classes and Eliza Fox, also Octavia Hill were volunteer teachers. Barbara Leigh Smith formed a committee with the intention of changing the law, in order to give a married woman the right to her own property. In effect, a woman gave up the right to her own income and possessions when she married. The group raised a petition to Parliament in 1856 enlisting the support of the leading writers of the day. Elizabeth Barrett Browning, Marian Evans, Mary Howitt, J. S. Mill, Harriet Taylor, and Mrs Gaskell, were amongst the thousands who signed the petition. It was not until 1870 that the Married Women's Property Act allowed married women to retain their own inheritance or earnings.

Wm Havell- Temple of Vesta, Tivoli

~ CATALOGUE OF WORKS ~

DATE	TITLE	Cms		EXH	SALES
1848	Portrait of Henry Rose	18	15		
	Portait of Mrs Gilfroy	18	15		
1849	A View of Southampton	64	43		
	Calshot Castle/Dover Harb(pr)				B15/08/1996 lot224
	Pastoral-man chopping wood	74	61		
	Wooded River Landscape	68 diam			
	Mountns wooded l/s -trav by lake	58	48		S.21/7/78
	Entrance to port of Havre from Cucknor Hard				
1850	Portraits of Mr/s Day	18	15		
	The Temple of Vesta in Sabine Hills	125	86		C16/3/1973
	copy Spanish Landscape	71	58		
	Lago di Garda (poss 1860 date)	33	23		23/08/1994 Bristol
	Portait of E.Holder	76	63		C.24/5/2006
1851	River Scene nr Reading	41	36		
	A Bit in Berkshire	?		R.A. 1851	
	Figs in a peaceful lake ls nr waterfall	38	27		15/10/2001Sevenoaks
	Travellers on a highland road	45	30		25/03/1992 Sevenoaks
	Wooded landscape	58	48		C.21/7/78

Year	Title			Code
1852	Wooded L/S -gypsies by a river	109	69	C15/10/76
	Autumn Evening	76	64	
	English Landscape	64	48	
	The Herons Home	36	27	
	Fishing	25	20	
	Mother & child at edge of river	43	35	B25/11/92
	The ruined bridge	42	29	
1853	Munich	58	48	
	Break of day Botanic Garden Munich	34	28	
	Near Munich	39.5	28	
	River Scene-Rhine	91	53	C9/5/1891
	Earlymorn L Constance from Lindau	137	76	P30/11/1999
	Lake Constance from Bavarian side	127	89	
1854	Fishermans House,Bavaria	48	39	
	Fishermans Home Chiemsee Bavaria	65	52	
	Waiting to cross the Chiemsee Bavaria	63	47	
	The Frowen inlet on Chiemsee	85	52	
	In the Bavarian Mountains	32	23	
	Sunrise at Chiemsee Bavaria	34	21	
	In the Aust.Tyrol- (study)	72	48	
	Waterfall nr Altenmarkt Bavaria	65	46	
	L/s with figures	61	47	
	Morning Bavarian Highlands	71	46	

Storm at Portsmouth	58	44		
Oyster-smack aground Soton water	30	23		
1855 View nr Southampton	79	49		
Valley of the Inn,Munich	79	48		C.Apr 1890
Looking into Tyrol from Hoch Gern	39	33		
The Inn Valley at RingsReine Tyrol	127	89		
Nr Brannenburg Inn Valley U.Bavaria	81	51	LA 1856	06/12/1997 Cologne
Sunrise over Brannenburgh Bavaria	117	155	LA 1856	
Vineyards Meran Tyrol	79	48		
Fr Brannenburg in the Bavarian Highlands	58	49		
The Lake Chiemsee Bavaria	?		LA 1857	
Morning in hills of Tyrol	127	89		
Marriage festival Chiemsee	157	119	BI 1856	
Marriage festival Chiemsee	71	51		10/3/98
The coming storm Chiemsee	69	44		
Stormy day Bavarian Mountains	39	32		
Mountain storm in the Tyrol	68	56		
An Old Hermitage-borderland of Tyrol	79	63		
1856 Highland Loch Scene	94	69	B.I.1856	s. 9/9/75
Morning View on the Rhine				
Pine Forest on Fire	127	86		C. 23/5/65
Charcoal burner in the Wilde Kaiser mtns	124	107		
The Wilde-Kaiser Mountains	127	86	R.A.1856	C23/5/1865
Charcoal burner in the Wilde Kaiser mtns	127	89		C18/03/83
1856 The Wilde Kaiser	53	36		02/09/1998 Dublin

	The Wilde-Kaiser Mountains	79	48		
	Fortress Ehrenbreitstein	127	86	&w/c	
	The Blau Gumpa Rhine Valley	?		LA 1857	
	The Ripened Cornfield,Bavarian Highlands	?		LA 1858	
	Stone Pines,Tyrolean Frontier	?			
	Ave Maria at Bolzano	127	86	BI 1857	C13/10/2004
1857	Sunset on the Atlantic-Fr Portland Bill	?		LA 1857	
	Windmill nr Hythe	22	18		11/8/57
	The Spot King Rufus shot in New Forest	?		LA 1861	
	Grand sunrise Stonehenge	127	86		
	The Old Castle Jail	56	43		
	Old Wall Southampton	32	22		
	Sunny Day Derbyshire Hills	57	43	LA 1858	C.27/3/1876
	Lake Windemere	?			
	A View of Westmoreland	?			
	View in Cumberland-sunset	?			
	Matlock High Tor Derbyshire	?		LA 1858	
	Matlock Baths	?			
	Stone Pine, Matlock	?			
	Scraps in an atelier(oval)	90	72		09/06/2004 Doyle NY
1858	Temple of Venus	229	152		
	Lake Constance	1588	1200		
	Lake Constance above Lindau	1270	885	RA 1858	
	Lake Como (date ind)	1215	915		

88

	Lake Como from Moltrinzo	58	44	
	Italian Lake Scene (Lake Como)	91	61	
	Paestium	51	38	
	Early morning L Con from above Lindau	140	79	30/11/99
	A Chalet near Lake Como	46	35	P12/12/1989
	A Villa on shores of L Como			
	Wooded path shore L.Maggiore			
	Cypress Trees at Lake Como	46	25	B09/05/2000
	Storm on L.Como-study			
	Woody Heights ab. L.Como	127	86	
1859	Summer storm Roman campagna			
	Italian Scenery	50	38	
	Southern Euro I/s capprccio	24	18	
	Drawings from travels Sept/Oct			
	Mountainside Lakes&Rocks-study	52	35	
1859	The Coliseum (draft painting)	61	50	
	View of the Coliseum Rome	87	81	C 8/03/1862
1860	The Coliseum Rome	114	78	24/10/97+ S.7/6/1995
	The Coliseum by Moonlight	230	155	RA 1860
	The Temple of Vesta,Tivoli	128	90	
	The Tiber at Ponte Molle	?		
	Maecenas Villa towards Rome	?		

Quarry,Civita Castellana	54	38		
Etruscan tombs-Civita Castellan-Sunset	188	119		
The Grotto of Neptune	183	124	B.I.1860	
Temples at Agrigento	147	102		C.13/5/77
Tombs of the Scipios			B.I.1860	
Gt falls&temple of Sybil Tivoli	127	89		
River l/s with bargehorses	127	89		13/6/1989 Tennants
View in Tivoli	76	51		
A Classical Idyll	99	58		S.24/10/78
Neopolitan Landscape	119	74		
1861 Twilight in Abbadia Lariana	60	45		20/06/2005 S. Milan
View of the Regents Canal	48	37		
Evening	53	43		14/06/2001 Toronto
Whaling off Desolation Island	?	?	LA 1861	
Nemi- thespot where Aeneas landed	?	?	LA 1862	
Olive Groves at Varenna	226	152	RA+LSFA 1861	16/6/98
Pine Trees at Castel Fusano	183	124	B.I.1860	
The Villa D'Este Tivoli	188	119	B.I.1861/LA 1862	
Woods of Chestnut above Varenna	56	150	B.I.1861	Donated Tate1897
Lake Como,Sweet Chestnuts	53	35		
Varenna towards Swiss Mountains	127	76		C28/5/1865
Stone Pier Varenna- study	35	48		

Study Rocky foreground-L.Lecco				
Scene,Fiume Latte,L Lecco	76	56	BI/RA 1862	
Fiume Latte	30	23		14/03/2003 Detroit
1862				
The Temple of Saturn	127	89		
The Arch of Titus	127	89		
An Italianate Landscape shepherd/sheep	127	89		S2/2/79
Landscape in Alban Hills	127	89		C.9/10/1970
Tremezza Mountain.Menaggio	?		B.I. 1862	
Setting sun at Bolzano	?			C11/3/1863
The Cypress trees (in VID'este gardens)	?			C9/6/67
Monte Soracte-Roman Campagna	?		B.I.1863	
Pastoral Arcadia	27	37		S20/1/81
1863				
Early Morning	137	76		06/12/1998 Grogan
Evening mists-L Como	?		B.I. 1863	
Bellagio Rock on L.Como	152	61		
Bellagio Rock on L.Como	127	76		B.3/11/77
Round Pond Kensington Gdns	38	29		
Churchyard by the sea	53	37		02/12/2000 Germany
UNDATED				
Mountain Lake Landscape	155	78		C NY 15/06/1984
Italian Landscape with figure	48	25		7/12/00
Ventnor Isle of Wight	?			

Cottages Nr Ventnor	?		
Summer landscape	49	33	S16/03/88
Summer landscape	38	25	B28/02/85
Dido's return from a water excursion	127	76	S24/4/85
Acadian Landscape	26	20	
In the campagna	53	38	C13/6/1879
Portrait of boy by branch(one of pr)	25	15	25/05/1996 And&Garland
Southampton Water -Twilight	?		
Estuary at sunset	56	38	S21/7/82
Seashore-Ventnor	?		
Wooded hilly landscape	63	47	S 16/2/66
Shepherd with his flock	38	20	P.22/11/1982
Figs in Italianate l/scape	63	46	28/7/98
Cont lake l/c with figure and trees	46	25	6/3/01
Goatherder playing a pipe	54	38	C17/07/1998 I196
Faggot gatherers	50	33	C02/11/1989
The evening baths	29	21	
The passing cloud-calves and sheep grazing	61	50	
Rustic l/scape+bridge over stream(pair)	48	35	

Key

C   Christies. London   FAS Fine Art Society

B   Bonhams   LA Liverpool Academy

P   Phillips

S   Sothebys

~ BIBLIOGRAPHY ~

The Royal Academy of Arts. A Graves Graves & Co. London. 1905

The British Institution.1806-1867. Dictionary of Contributors. Graves

Epoch of Painting. Wornum. London. 1864. p544

Dictionary of Victorian Painters Christopher Wood 1971 illustrationp 15 p 219

Dictionary of National Biography Oxford Univ Press. Stephen & Lee. 1882

Victorian Painting. Reynolds. Herbert Press.1966 p155.

A Short History of Southampton.ed F.Clarke.Clarendon Press. 1910

A History of Southampton.1700-1914. Vol2. A. Patterson

Relics of Old Southampton. Loan Exhibition. 1904. Heasman Hartley Inst. Soton

The Grand Tour ed. Wilton and Bignamini. Tate Gallery. 1996

Ruskin Turner & Pre Raphaelites. Hewison Warrell and Wildman. Tate Gallery. 2000

Ruskins Artists. Hewison. Ashgate Pub. 2000

Ruskin. The Early Years. Hilton. Yale Univ. Press &London. 1985

Ruskin and the Brownings: 25 unpublished letters. ed D. DeLaura. John Rylands Library.
    1972

Modern Painters.Vol 2. Ruskin. Dent & Sons. 1930.

The Lamp of Beauty:Writings on Art. Ruskin.Phaidon Press. 1959

British Romanticism. Curran. Cambridge Univ Press. 1993

The Grand Tour Hudson Folio Society. 1993

The Grand Tour R.S.Lambert. Faber & Faber. 1935

Turner on Tour. Inge Herold. Pegasus Library Prestel. 1997

Italy in The Age of Turner. C. Powell. London. Merrell Holberton. 1998

Turners Classical Landscapes. Nicholson. Princeton. 1990

Letters from Italy. J. T. Headley. Wiley and Putnams. Library of American Books. 1845

The Fortunate Pilgrims. Baker. Harvard Univ Press. 1964

Handlist of Painters, Sculptors and Architects associated with St Marylebone 1760-1960.
    Bor. of St Marylebone Public Libraries.1963 Ann Cox-Johnson.

Reminiscences of my Life. Holiday. W. Heinemann. 1914

Old Water Colour Society's Club Annual 1963. Centenary Memoir of J. D. Harding by C.
    Skilton.

History of the Old Water-Colour Society..J. L. Roget.Longmans Green & Co.1891

Principles and Practice of Art. J. D. Harding. Chapman & Hall. 1845

The Royal Academy Review by the Council of Four. 1860. Kent & Co.

William Havell.1782-1857. Owen. Reading Museum and Art Gallery. 1981
Diary of Ford Madox Brown. Ed. V. Surtees. Yale University Press. 1981
Gambart. Prince of the Victorian Art World. Maas Barrie & Jenkins Ltd. 1975.
The Victorian Art World in Photographs. Maas. Barrie & Jenkins Ltd. 1984
Leaves from a Life. Panton. Eveleigh Nash. 1908.
W. H. Bartlett. A. Ross Univ. Toronto Press. 1973
W.H. Bartlett. J. Britton Bradbury & Evans. 1855
The Liverpool School of Painters. Marillier. Murray. 1904
The Royal Watercolour Society. Woodbridge. 1992
The Letters of Mrs Gaskell. J. A. V. Chapple and A Pollard. Manchester Univ. Press. 1966
Further Letters of Mrs Gaskell. Chapple and Shelston. Manchester Univ Press. 2000
Passages from the French and Italian Notebooks of Nathaniel Hawthorne. Strahan & Co. 1871
Notes in England and Italy. Mrs Hawthorne. Putnam. 1869
Painting Women. Victorian Women Artists. Cherry. Routledge. 1993.
English Female Artists. E. C. Clayton. Tinsley Bros. 1876 p80
A Victorian Canvas. ed. N. Wallis. G Bles. London. 1957
Barbara Leigh Smith Bodichon. 1827-1891. P. Hirsch. Chatton & Windus. 1998
Argosy. Feb 1890. Article by E. Bridell-Fox
Memories. A Girl's Own Paper 19/7/1890 p657
Elizabeth Barrett-Browning. Letters to Her Sister 1846-1859. Huxley. Murray. 1929
The Letters of Elizabeth Barrett Browning to her sister Arabella. Ed. S. Lewis. Wedgestone Press. 2002
Life and Death of Elizabeth Barrett-Browning: R. Browning. Florence. 30/6/1861
Sir Charles Eastlake and The Victorian Art World. Robertson Princeton University Press 1978.
Journal and Corresp. of Lady Eastlake ed. by C. E. Smith. Murray. 1895
Richard P. Bonington. M. Cormack. Phaidon. 1989
The Life of W. J. Fox. Dr. Garnett. John Lane. London. 1910
The Dickens Circle. J. W. T. Ley. London. 1918

Articles

Southampton Times and Hampshire Express 14/1 & 21/1/88
An Appreciation by WB Hill 1917 – Coliseum by Moonlight.
Hants Advertiser and Soton Times 7/12/29
Southern Daily Echo 13/4/49
Christopher Wood 1971 p15
Burlington Magazine dec 1968 P719 revue of Sheffield exhibition.
Apollo Aug 1974 Bridell and Romantic Landscape. J Sweetman
Southampton Art Gallery Catalogue series 1 May 1975
The Gaskell Society Journal 5 1991 E. Fox by Brenda Colloms